THE BANK OF FAITH;

OR,

A LIFE OF TRUST

by

WILLIAM HUNTINGTON, S.S.

Minister of Providence Chapel, London

Abridged and Revised by

William McDonald

Second President of the
National Campmeeting Association for the Promotion of Holiness

"And he said unto them, When I sent you without purse, and scrip, and shoes, lacked ye anything? And they said, Nothing"
(Luke xxii:35).

SCHMUL
PUBLISHING

This Schmul Publishing Co. edition is not a scanned facsimile of a used book. It has not been "updated" or edited into modern English, punctuation or grammar, but is accurate to the author's own style and usage. The text has been carefully proofread for accuracy and formatted for easier reading by today's readers. Every effort has been made to prevent disordered text.

Published by Schmul Publishing Co.
PO Box 776
Nicholasville, KY 40340

ISBN 10: 0-88019-676-9
ISBN 13: 978-0-88019-676-5

Visit us on the Internet at wesleyanbooks.com, or order direct from the publisher by calling 800-772-6657, or by writing to the above address.

Contents

ZION'S BANK.

As Sung by Rev. G. W. Anderson.   Arr. by Joshua Gill.

1.　　I have a never-failing bank, Well fill'd with golden store;
2. The notes that are accepted here, With blood must all be signed;
3.　　A lep-er had a little note, Lord, if thou wilt, thou can:
4. Some fear they write so poor a hand, Their notes will be rejected;
5. Sometimes my banker smiling says, Why don't you oftener come;
6.　　Richer and richer still I grow, The poor-er I be - come;

No other bank contains so much That can enrich the poor.
All others, bear what name they may, Are ut-ter-ly de-clined.
The banker cash'd his little note, And sav'd the wretched man.
But always humble souls obtain Much more than they expected.
And when I draw a little note, Why not a lar-ger one?
And thus for-ev-er it will be, Till I ar-rive at Home!

CHORUS.

O, there's a plen-ty, a plen-ty, a plen-ty:

O, there's a plen-ty in Fa-ther's Bank a-bove.

Introduction

"THE BANK OF FAITH," which we here introduce to our readers, will be found helpful to such as believe that "all things are possible to him that believeth." The subject of faith for temporal matters has failed to secure the attention which it demands. The author of "The Bank of Faith" well exemplifies the subject, whose whole life seems to have been a life of trust. In many respects he was a unique character, but in the matter of faith he was eminently scriptural. The artless simplicity with which he relates the simple story of his trust in God for temporal supply, carries conviction to every Christian heart. A man with no educational advantages, his mission was to the poor. But the educated and wealthy, whose hearts had been touched by the grace of God, listened to him with delight. "I believe," he says, "God never intended me to be a preacher to the rich, because He has ever kept me dependent on His providence. Had I been rich, I might have been tempted to trust in uncertain riches; and I know well that 'where the treasure is, there will the heart be also.' Nor have I any reason to believe that God ever intended me for a preacher to please Pharisees." He was an earnest, spiritual man. "By nature," he says, "we are all fond of a specious form of religion, and God permitted me to use a dry form for many years; but He never regarded any of those prayers put up by me, nor removed the guilt of my sin in answer to them; therefore, to use an English proverb, 'I shall never speak well of that bridge, because it never bore me safe over the stream.'"

Mr. Huntington is very severe on formalism. "I know," he says "that God tells us to turn away from those who 'have a form of godliness, but deny the power thereof.' And dry forms of devotion, used by people who deny the grace and Spirit of God, are no better than a stage for antichrist, a varnish for sepulchres (Matt. xxiii. 27); an apparel for harlots (Isa. iv. 1); a winding sheet for Pharisees (Isa. xxx. 1); a bribe of dead works put into the hands of an honest conscience (Heb. ix. 14); a trading stock for blind guides (Isa. lvi. 11); a dish of husks to stifle convictions (Luke xv. 16); a mongrel service offered to God and Mammon (Matt. vi. 24); the mimicry of hypocrites (Matt. xv. 8); a starting hole to shun the cross (Isa. xliii. 22); and infidelity's last refuge.

"God permitted me, for many years, to try what a form of devotion would do for me; but, like the poor woman in the gospel, I got worse instead of better, therefore was obliged to lay it by, and let the words of my mouth be the meditations of my heart."

When Mr. Huntington had become fully disenthralled from the bondage of formalism, the question of life of trust was presented to his mind, and he soon accepted it as the will of God. "I believe God intended," he says, "that I should preach *faith*, because He has kept me dependent by faith on Himself both for spiritual and temporal supplies." While his faith did not aspire to great undertakings, it was none the less clear, scriptural and effective. His temporal wants were not extravagant, but such as they were, God supplied them in answer to prayer. And he assigns as a reason for writing his "Bank of Faith" that "we are often tempted to believe that God takes no notice of our temporal concerns."

Mr. Huntington as firmly believed that his mission was to the poor as that he was required to live by faith. "I am persuaded," he says, "that God intended me for a minister to the *ignorant* and to the *poor:* to the ignorant, because he sent me to preach, and gave me many seals to my ministry before I could read a chapter in the Bible with priority; to the poor, because he sent me without a penny in my pocket, therefore, as a minister to the poor, I hope to magnify my office."

"The Bank of Faith," when first published, met with no little opposition, as did its author. He says, "I did not expect that it would be in equal esteem with the Bank of England." He was "aware of the reproach which would be cast upon such a work, as also upon the author, but this does in no wise concern me." He says, "I only wish that I was as free from every sin as I am from the carnal fear of man." He expresses the belief, that, "if Elijah were on earth, he would be loaded with as many reproaches of uncharitableness as I have been. But why should I wonder at this, when Christ Himself was accused by the doctors of old of preaching and working under the influence of a bad spirit." "The Bank of Faith," he says, "has dropped into the hands of these gentlemen, and it has acted the part of Samson; that is, it has made sport for them. And no wonder, seeing they have attributed the government of the world to blind fortune, and the glory which is due to God is ascribed to a phantom on a wheel." And yet these men are said to have been ministers of the gospel.

Having said so much in regard to the author of "The Bank of Faith," we must refer the reader to the work itself for further information. We have revised the work for further information. We have revised the work, omitting those portions which seemed to us of little value, and adapting it to the modern reader. The work has been out of print for some years, and, when published, was in such an unattractive style as to turn the ordinary reader away from its perusal.

We believe that the subject of faith for temporal as well as spiritual blessings should be revived in the Church. On every side the cry rings out, "work!" "work!" "work!" To this we have no objection, provided it be the "work of faith." To this end, it must spring from faith. But it is very certain that most of the work done is that of "going about to establish our own righteousness." It does not spring from a living faith, which "works by love and purifies the heart."

The soul's need should be supplied by faith. This is paramount to all else. We are "*justified* by faith," and "have peace with God." After this, the heart is "purified by faith," and our "love is made perfect." We are then "kept by the power of God through faith." So that every step in the soul's progress is secured and maintained by faith.

The body has its needs as well as the soul, and these are to be under the law of faith. While we are not to sit down and vainly trust God to feed us in our indolence, we are to remember that our resources are limited without the interposition of God. And we are to trust God for temporal supplies as truly as for spiritual, as God is the author of both.

Where our resources fail, the divine supply may be looked up for. The *oil* and the *flour* did not multiply while there was any left in the *cruse* or the *barrel*. But when the widow had reached the bottom of both, then God came to her help in answer to the prayer of the prophet. It is not a difficult task to trust God for bread with a full barrel to draw from. But the place to try our faith is over an *empty* barrel. The author of "The Bank of Faith" was successful at times, as the reader will learn by perusal of the following pages.

If the body is sick, and human skill fails to heal, we are to remember that Jesus can heal the body as well as the soul. To Him we are to make our appeal when human skill can render us no valuable aid.

Mr. Wesley records in his journal many cases in point: "When I came home, they told me the physician said he did not expect Mr. Myrick would live till morning. I went to him, but his pulse was gone. He had been speechless and senseless for some time. A few of us immediately joined in prayer. (I relate the naked fact.) Before we had done, his sense and his speech returned. Now, he that will account for this, by natural causes, has my free leave; but I choose to say, 'This is the power of God."

"I was desired," he says, "to visit one who was eminently pious, but had now been confined to her bed for several months, and was utterly unable to raise herself up. She desired us to pray that the chain might be broken. A few of us prayed in faith. Presently she rose up, dressed herself, came down stairs, and I believe had no further complaint."

Our one desire in sending "The Bank of Faith" in this form on its mission is, to help the faith of God's poor children according to His Word.

W. McDonald.
Boston, Mass.

Chapter 1.

WHEN I WAS ABOUT seven years of age I heard a person say that God took notice of children's sins. The wonderful workings of my mind upon these words I shall not at present describe; neither shall I mention the many trails I underwent at the bar of my own conscience, while the impression dwelt on my mind. I also remember to have once heard a person say that all things were possible with God; which words I secretly treasured up and pondered in my heart; and as I had great desire at that time to live in the capacity of an errand-boy with a certain gentleman in the place, being very poorly brought up, and knowing much the want of the common necessaries of life, it came into my mind that, if all things were possible with God, it was also possible for him to send me to live as a servant-boy with Squire Cook; though at the same time he had a boy who I believed was well approved of. Notwithstanding this last circumstance, I privately asked God, in an extempore way, to give me that boy's place; and made many promises how good I would be if he granted me this request. For many days I privately begged of God this favor, which nobody knew but God and myself, till now I relate it. I believe I went on in this way of praying, sometimes under a hedge, or on my bed, for a week or two; and I thought, if God granted me this favor, I should know whether all things were possible with him or not. Having prayed for many days, and finding no likelihood of an answer, I readily concluded that there was no God; and therefore I had no cause to be so afraid of sinning, nor I any occasion to pray to him any more. Accordingly I left off praying for some time, and then began again, till at last I left off entirely. Some few days after this, there came a man to my father's house, and said, "William, Squire Cooke wants a boy, why don't you go after the place?" I said, "John Dungy lives there." He answered, "No, he is turned away." I asked for what. He replied, "Old Master Coly, the oyster-man, went there a few days ago, to carry some oysters and, while the old man was gone with a measure of them into the house, the boy robbed the pads, as they hung on the horse, while he was tied at the gate and the mistress, seeing him, discharged him for it."

The compunction which I felt, the thoughts that I had, the various workings of my mind, the promises I made, and the petitions I put up, as I went after the place, I choose to conceal; for I think they would hardly be credited, considering I was no more, at this time, than eight years old. However, to my astonishment, I got the place, and the bargain was struck at twenty shillings per annum. For many days and weeks an uncommon impression about the power of God lay fresh on my mind. But, soon after this, a sudden temptation brought me to believe that there was no God; that, if there was, he took no notice of such creatures as we are, or of any of our affairs; and that it was by chance I got the place; wherefore I imagined that I had no occasion to pray, or to pay the vows which I had made. This temptation made a sufficient breach for me to creep out at, and proved an awful inlet to vice and vanity, which for some months I gave way to. Soon after this, I offended my master, was discharged from my servitude, and went home as deeply stung with guilt for my folly as I had been before lifted up at the sight of God's mercy.

After this period I had sharp work in my conscience for some years, at certain times, but was still pursued with deistical principles—that God took no notice of our proceedings; till at last it appeared rather fixed in my mind, and insensibility and stupor naturally followed. Now it was that I got wholly out of all fear of God, or thoughts of futurity, and very soon learned to dance; which is just as serviceable a net to ruin souls as devils could invent, or frail mortals drop into. However, God put a stop to this, by laying a fit of sickness in my tabernacle, which I had never before experienced. I labored hard, rather than submit to go to bed, and made a shift to keep about my business as long as I was able to move a limb; but at last I was forced to yield. Then my conscience began to perform her office, and the wrath of God to alarm me; so that I was fully convinced God took notice of my conduct in this life, and would reckon with me for it in the next. I lay in this state of mind until I had an earnest of damnation in my heart, and I had not a single doubt of my portion in everlasting burnings, if I died in that state. God brought me so nigh the end of all flesh that the rattles of death stopped my breath twice. I tried to fly from death, and got out of the bed to run away, but could not; for I fell on the floor, and there lay till my fellow-servants found me, and put me into bed again by force. Soon after I heard one of the maids say, "Poor William will die." "Yea," said the other, "Doctor Wilson has given him over." They knew not that I heard them. I tried again to fly from death, but found I could not. So I began to whisper a prayer to God, which conscience would not allow me to do before. As I began to pray, I gathered strength, and in less than a month was out of doors. I quitted my servitude, went home to my parents till my recovery, and never danced any more from that hour to this. Soon after I got well I was informed that one 'Squire Pool, of Charren in Kent, wanted a servant. I went after the place, and took courage to ask of God the favor of success, as he had been pleased to punish me for my past folly, and had brought me to believe that I had highly offended him. I went under a hedge, and put up a solemn prayer to him to give me success in my journey, and make me an object of his care for the future. I cut a stick half through, and bent it down in the hedge which I promised to look at, on my return, and render praise to God, if he granted me this favor. Somewhat like poor Jacob, in his trouble, when he anointed the pillar, by pouring a little oil upon the top of it; and promising, if God would keep him, then he should be his God, and, of all that God should give him, he would give God the tenth part. God heard my prayer, and I got the place. Though there was a servant in the parlor with the gentleman, and though they had partly agreed when I went in, yet he broke off the bargain with him to my astonishment. The reason why he chose me in preference to the other was, because he was a married man and I was not. This was the *secondary* cause; but I resolved it by the *primary* one. At my return, I looked with many tears at the sick which I had marked, and offered up an imperfect tribute of praise to the God of my daily mercies, whom I had neglected and much offended.

For some time I endeavored, while in place, to walk so as to please God, as I imagined; but alas! the vanities of this world are too strong for any but those "who are kept, by the mighty power of God, through faith unto salvation;" which power I knew nothing of, therefore my resolutions were soon broken, and I forgot my God. But soon after this he again put his afflicting hand on me, and laid me on a sick bed for many months; nor did I recover effectually for three years after. But still distress of mind, at times, followed me, and, blessed be God, he did not wholly leave me without some convictions, till he brought me to know the truth as it is in Jesus. One particular instance of Providence I here recollect also; which was, I had ordered my box of clothes to be left at the Star Inn at Maid-Stone in Kent, for the Cranbrook carrier to bring to me; but he said it was not there. So I went to search after it, fearing it was lost. At this time I was so poor in the pocket that I had but one shilling left in all the world. However, I thought I should be able to go out and return again in one day, therefore that shilling would bear my charges; but, when I came to Maid-Stone, the box was not there. I was obliged to go farther; and, in my return, I found myself so weak and low that I could not get back that day. The shilling was gone, my strength was gone, and the weather was very wet and cold; night, too, began to draw on apace, and at this time I was two miles from Maid-Stone, which was fourteen from Cranbrook. While I was thinking of, and mourning over, my miserable situation, I thought if I were one that feared and loved God, as others in olden time had done, I might have any thing at his hands; but as for me, I had made him my enemy by sin, and therefore he would take no notice of me, nor of anybody else, in our days, for parsons and people were all wicked alike. Presently after this came suddenly on my mind to go out of the foot-path, which led through the fields, to go into the horse-road, though at the same time the foot-path was by far the best. I had been in the road scarcely a minute before I cast my eye on the ground, and there lay a sixpence. I took it up, and before I had walked many steps farther, there lay a shilling also. I took that up, and it supplied my necessities at that time. These manifold providences and answers to prayer, did, at times, deeply impress my mind that God had some regard for me; but when sin was committed all these thoughts were blasted.

However, I never could entirely, after this time, get rid of all my thoughts about the awful day of judgement—the dreadful consideration of an endless eternity—the tremendous tribunal of God—the woeful state of a guilty sinner before him—the certain conquest of triumphant death and certain approach to God's bar—the wretched figure that a guilty soul would make when all his secret and open sins were exposed to God, angels, and men,—and the miserable punishment which souls must feel who have their doom fixed in the gloomy receptable of the damned; these things were, at times, uppermost in my thoughts; and though I pursued many pleasures in order to stifle them, yet I had felt enough to fix a lasting conviction of the truth of them upon my soul.

Having wandered about for some years in this solitary way, "seeking rest and finding none," it happened that I once went to work at Darnbury Park, in Essex, for one 'Squire Fitch. I had been there but a few days before I fell sick, and was carried to the sign of the Bell, where nobody knew me, and with only two shillings in my pocket; but Providence sent an old widow, whose name was Shepherd, and whose deceased husband had been a butcher. This woman, being much of a doctress, doctored me, nursed me, watched with me, and fed me, though she never saw me before or since, nor had she anything for her trouble, and yet took as much care of me as if I had been her own child. A few years ago I was determined to go down and see her, and restore her fourfold for her labor, and tell her what God had done for me; but, upon inquiry, I found that she had been dead about three months before my arrival.

I do not remember any other particular providence until I was married, when my wife and I took ready-furnished lodgings at Mortlake, in Surrey, where God smote my conscience effectually. It so happened that I fell lame, having received a wrench in my loins, which rendered me incapable of labor for many days. During this time our money was all gone, and we were but strangers in the place, having been in it but about half a year. After I began to recover a little, there fell a deep snow on the ground, which prevented my working for many days. Here Providence suffered us to know what it was to want. We had one child, about five or six months old, which was our first-born. It happened one morning early that my wife asked me for the tinder-box, seemingly in a great fright, crying out, "I wonder the poor child has not waked all night." She lighted the candle and took up the child; and behold it was dead, and as black as a coal! It went off in a convulsive fit, as five more had done since, all of whom turned black also. Here Providence appeared again; for, about three or four months before this death happened, a gentleman, in whose garden I at times had wrought, desired me to look after his horse in the country while he was in town, for which I was to have one shilling per week. The very day on which the child died the gentleman came down from London, and I got my money of him for looking after the horse, which just served to bury the poor infant. My lameness, poverty, distress of mind, the sufferings of my wife, loss of my child, and the sense of God's wrath, were the most complicated distresses I had ever felt. From this time spiritual convictions began to plough so deep in my heart as to make way for the word of eternal life; which brought me experimentally to know "the only true God, and Jesus Christ, whom he hath sent." And if God should spare my life, and give me time, I may acquaint the world of the whole dealings of God with my soul in a treatise by itself; but in this I intend treating chiefly of the providence of God, lest the book swell too big for the poor to purchase.

I do not remember any particular providence attending me till about three or four years after, when I was brought savingly to believe in Jesus Christ for life and salvation. At this time I dwelt in a ready-furnished lodging at Sunbury in Middlesex, where my eldest daughter, now living, fell sick at about five or six months old, and was wasted to a skeleton. We had a doctor to attend her, but she got worse and worse. Having lost our first child, this was a dear idol to us; and I suppose it lay as near my heart as poor Isaac did to the heart of Abraham. However, it appeared as if God was determined to bereave us of her, for he brought her even to death's door. My wife and I have sat up with her night after night, watching the cradle, expecting every breath to be her last, for two or three weeks together. At last I asked the doctor if he thought there was any hope for her life. He answered, No; he would not flatter me; she would surely die. This distressed me beyond measure; and, as he told me he could do no more for her, I left my lodging-room, went to my garden in the evening, and in my little tool-house wrestled hard with God in prayer for the life of the child; but upon these conditions: that if my request was granted, and she should live to arrive at the full stature in life, and in future times turn wicked, and be damned for sin, and that my earnest prayer should be the cause of it, I besought God not to regard my petition for the child, though she was as dear to me as my own life. I went home satisfied that God had heard me, and in three days the child was as well as she is now, and ate as heartily, only her flesh was not perfectly restored. This effectually convinced me that all things were possible with God.

Chapter II.

I HAD NOW DWELT about fourteen months at Sunbury, and had served a gentleman in the capacity of a gardener at twelve shillings per week. The gentleman informed me he purposed to keep his carriage, and intended that his driver should work in the garden; therefore he should only hire a man now and then a day, but should not keep a gardener constantly. I was, in consequence, discharged from my work; but had the liberty offered me of staying till I could get employment elsewhere. I believe my master often saw the felicity of my mind, and the wisdom that God had given me by the answers I was enabled to give to his various questions. Grace carries many rays of majesty with it, though it take up its abode in a beggar. However, I thought this world was his god, therefore I refused his offer, as Abraham did the present that was offered him by the king of Sodom; that is I would take nothing that was his, "from a thread even to a shoe latchet."

After I had been three weeks out of employment I heard of a place at Ewell, in Surrey; which I went after, and engaged in. It was with a gentleman that manufactured gunpowder. I agreed for eleven shillings per week in the summer, and ten shillings in the winter; and procured a ready-furnished room in an old thatched house on Ewell-Marsh (if with propriety it might be called a furnished room) at two shillings a week. I was obliged to pawn all my best clothes in order to defray our expenses, owing to me being out of employment, and to hire a cart to carry my personal effects (which were but few) to Ewell. When the cart set us down on Ewell-Marsh, on Monday morning, and I had paid the hire of it, I had the total sum of tenpence halfpenny left, to provide for myself, my wife and child, till the ensuing Saturday night! But though I were thus poor, yet I knew God had made me rich in faith; and these words came on my mind with power: "He multiplied the loaves and fishes to feed five thousand men, besides women and children." We went on our knees, and turned the account of that miracle into prayer, beseeching the Almighty to multiply what we had or to send relief another way, as his infinite wisdom thought most proper. The next evening my landlord's daughter and son-in-law came up to see their mother, with whom I lodged, and brought some baked meat, which they had just taken out of their oven, and brought for me and my wife to sup along with them. These poor people knew nothing of us, nor of our God. The next day in the evening they did the same, and kept sending victuals or garden stuff to us all week long. We had not made our case known to any but God; nor did we appear ragged, or like people in want, no, we appeared better in dress than even those who relieved us; but God sent an answer to our prayer by them, who knew not at the same time what they were about, nor did I tell them till some months after. While we were at supper, I entertained them with spiritual conversation. After supper I went to prayer with them, and prayed most earnestly for them. And God answered it; for he sent the woman home deeply convicted that night; nor did her convictions abate till she was brought to see Christ crucified in the open vision of gospel faith, and to receive peace and pardon from Christ for herself. Some time after this God began to work upon the husband also; and then I related the fore-cited circumstance, at the hearing of which he told how it was impressed on his mind that I was in want of victuals, and his wife found fault with him for thinking so, and bringing it to me, saying, "The people are better to pass than we are." But he contradicted her, and insisted on her doing as he desired.

I found that the small pittance of eleven shillings per week (as I paid two shillings for a ready-furnished lodging) would amount very slowly towards getting my clothes out of the pawn, which, with the interest, amounted to near forty shillings, and which I was loath to lose. It came into my mind to search my Bible, to see if any instruction for faith could be got about this matter. I turned to these words, "There is a lad here which hath five barley loaves and two fishes; but what are they among so many?" I asked my wife if she had ever ate barley bread. She said, "Yes, in Dorsetshire." I told her I never had eaten it, but the poor Saviour and his apostles had; and I supposed it was because (speaking after the manner of men) they could get no better food. And, as God saw it necessary to keep us in a state of deep poverty, it ill became us to complain, or to refuse the meanest diet, seeing he had blessed us with an assured hope of heaven hereafter. She said she was willing if I was. So she went to a farmer to ask him to sell her a bushel of barley. His reply was, that he sold his barley by the quarter, or load, to malsters for making malt; and should not trouble himself with measuring such a small quantity. So she went to a corn-chandler in Ewell, and asked for the same article, whose answer was, "I have only the refuse of the barley, or tail corn, which I sell for swine and fowls." My wife told him that would do; but did not inform him for what use it was intended. This was ground at the mill, and was very cordially received by us, as the love of God, which we enjoyed in our hearts, more than counterbalanced all the poverty we labored under; for I well knew it was decreed by God himself that his people should have tribulation in this world, but in Christ Jesus they should have peace. And love made the yoke easy and the burden light; for, if at any time a murmuring thought entered my mind, it was soon quelled by considering that Christ lived on the alms of his poor followers, and that he was worse off than either the foxes or the birds. As it is written, "The foxes have holes, and the birds of the air have nests, but the Son of man hath not where to lay his head." This has often made my heart yearn within me, silenced all my murmurings, and dissolved my soul in gospel gratitude.

My wife and I now kept house at a very cheap rate: two shillings and sixpence per week carried us through tolerably well. As for the world's dainties, we were satisfied without them; for we knew that the grace of God had enabled us to choose that good part which shall never be taken from us, therefore patience had, in a manner, her perfect work. We soon saved upwards of twenty shillings, with which, on the Saturday night, I set off to Kingston to get some of my clothes out of pawn, leaving money on the hands of my wife to get half a bushel of barley. It so happened that the apparel which I went to redeem came to so much, with the interest, that I had not enough money left to bring home. This was a great trial to us, because our poor little girl, who had been but lately weaned, had nothing to carry her through the week but bare barley cakes; and, though she would eat barley, yet I could not endure to see her live on that only. On the Monday following I went heavily to work, and very much distressed to know how my poor little one was to live. I reflected with indignation on myself for parting with my money, thinking I had better have gone without my clothes than have exposed my poor little one to want the necessaries of life. But, as I went over a bridge that led to my work, I cast my eye on the right hand side, and there lay a very large eel on the mud by the river side, apparently dead. I caught hold of it, and soon found it was only asleep. With difficulty I got it safe out of the mud upon the grass, and then carried it home. My little one was very fond of it, and it richly supplied all her wants that day. But at night I was informed that the eel was all gone, so the next day afforded me the same distress and trouble as the preceding day had done. When going to my work, cruelly reflecting on myself for parting with all my money, just as I entered the garden gates I saw a partridge lie dead on the walk. I took it up, and found it warm. I carried it home, and it richly supplied the table of our little one that day. A few days after this my master told me he had found a partridge on the garden walk also, but it had stunk. I told him I had found one a little before that time. He said that two males had been fighting, and had killed each other, which was very common. But I was enabled to look higher.

Carnal reason always traces everything from God to second causes, and there leaves them floating upon uncertainties; but faith traces them up to their first cause, and fixes them there; by which means God's hand is known, and himself glorified. I believe this battle between the plumed warriors was proclaimed by the Lord; for, if a sparrow falls not to the ground without God's leave (as the scriptures declare), I can hardly think a partridge does.

The third day arrived, and I was still in the same case as before. As I went to my work I saw the bird's nest in one of the shrubs; which, upon examination, I found to be the nest of a large bird, with four young ones in it, just ready to fly. It was with much reluctance I stormed and plundered the little simple citadel—but necessity hath no law, therefore I was forced to rob the poor dam of her young, and leave her mourning and lamenting, while my young one lived upon hers.

However, I found it was no sin in God's sight. "If a bird's nest chance to be before thee in the way in any tree, or on the ground, whether they be young ones or eggs, and the dam sitting upon the young ones or upon the eggs, thou shalt not take the dam with the young; but thou shalt in any wise let the dam go, and take the young to thee, that it may be well with thee, and that thou mayest prolong thy days" (Deut. xxii. 6, 7).

These birds served for that day very well; but the next day found me still unprovided as before, and brought forth fresh work for faith and prayer. However, the morrow still took thought for the things of itself; for, when I came to take the scythe in my hand to mow the short grass, I looked into the pond, and there I saw three very large carp lying on the water, apparently sick. When my master came to me I told him of it. He went and looked, and said they were dead; and told me I might have them, if I would, for they were not in season. However, they came in due season to me. And I found, morning after morning, there lay two or three of these fish at a time, dead, just as I wanted them; till I believe there was not one live fish remaining, six inches long, in that pond, which was near three hundred feet in length.

While musing on, and admiring the tender care of my God in his providence, and wondering what could move him thus to pity such a sinner, who was so unworthy of his grace, mercy and truth, as well as of his providential regard, these words came to my mind: "He turned their water into blood, and slew their fish" (Ps. cv, 39). My master told me he thought it was the heat of the sun that killed them, and I believe it was; but I knew that the sun and his heat were both from God, and that the sun shined in due season for me. And it much amazed me to see God so kind, even in temporal matters. It led me to search his blessed Word for similar circumstances. And, when I read of the distress and simple covenant of Jacob, of God's changing the color of Laban's cattle, that they might change their master, and of God's blessing his simple means of peeling the rods, that the pregnant dams might look at them and bring forth accordingly, and so setting the dams a longing to bring forth a motley progeny like the rods, which he set in the troughs, and the dream of the speckled ram begetting spotted inheritance of faith, I could not help weeping and admiring the unmerited goodness of my God in setting the birds of the air to war, sending the sunbeams with such a hostile force as to slay the inhabitants of the floods, suffering the eel to sleep till the hand of the necessitous had entangled him, and directing my eyes to the little lodgment of birds when all other supplies seemed to be cut off. It so operated on my mind that I cannot describe the humility, compunction, love, joy, and peace, which I felt. Oh, the goodness of God to the children of men! I evidently saw that, both in providence and grace, God is the same to us as he was to the saints in days of old, and that they had no preeminence over us in the covenant of grace at all; but that Jesus Christ was the same yesterday that he is to-day, and will be the same for ever. Let not these providences beget a notion in the weak of the flock of any partiality in God to me in particular, knowing that "God is no respecter of persons; but in every nation those that fear him and work righteousness are accepted of him."

I found that my pay would hardly support my family with comfort, and it came into my mind that I could mend shoes if I tried. I accordingly sent my wife to Kingston to buy me some materials for the business; upon which I began, and made a decent proficient in a very little time. This helped me so much that I got all my things out of the pawn, and kept myself entirely out of debt. But it happened one night that my wife complained to me that she had nothing for the child but barley cake. I told her I had a job of cobbling to do, and would sit up that night to finish it, that in the morning the work might be carried home, when peradventure she might get the money. So we sat up and worked together till between eleven and twelve o'clock, when I heard a person call at my window. I went down, and found several men on horseback (to appearance they were smugglers), who inquired their way to Malden Mills. I went a little way to show them, for which one of them gave me a shilling. On receiving it my very hair moved upon my head at the reflection of the daily providences of God. I mention this because God says that the gold and silver are his, that it is he only who maketh poor and maketh rich, and that it is he who bringeth low and lifteth up. These things so endeared God to me that I often called him my Bank, my Banker, and my blessed Overseer; and earnestly begged that he would condescend to be my tutor, my master, and my provider and never leave me in the hands of mortals, either for tuition, protection, or for temporal supplies. I no longer envied the rich in this world; for, if they are gracious, they only see one side of God's face, having an independent stock in hand; and, if graceless, they are of all flesh the most miserable. I clearly perceived that the most eminent saints in the Bible were brought into low circumstances, as Jacob, David, Moses, Joseph, Job, and Jeremiah, and all the apostles, in order that the hand of providence might be watched.

When harvest came on, my wife informed me that she should go to gleaning, in order to pick up some wheat to make bread with. So we generally arose about three o'clock in the morning, and I gleaned with her till six, and then went to my work; but she continued till eight o'clock, then went home with her corn, ate her breakfast, got the child up from bed (which all this time had been left alone), and then she went off for the day. At this time I had begun to preach at Ewell Marsh, which made no small stir that way; therefore the farmers drove my wife out of the fields, and the gleaners came about her like a shoal of small birds attending the funeral of a dead hawk, swearing that parson's wives should not glean there. "What," said they, "wives of the clergy go a gleaning!" I own it is not a good sign nor a good sight to see Levites gleaning; but, if the blind guides steal the offerings of God, which should feed the Levites, the Levites then must work or starve.

In Scripture a gospel minister is compared to an ox, so that he must take Christ's yoke, and learn to draw; and, when his day's work is ended, he must tread out the corn, if required; and, if God uses him to plough up the fallow ground of the heart, he must expect to work hard and fare hard. To be a gospel laborer is a rare thing, but to be a dumb dog, to lie at the bone and forget to bark, is very common. We read in Scriptures of the oxen ploughing while the asses were feeding beside them (Job. I., 14). But still God's hand was seen; for, if they drove her out of one field, she was surely directed into another, where she often found them carrying the corn, and then she got the first and prime gleanings of the whole field. At six o'clock I went in search after her, and gleaned with her till nine, or as long as we could see an ear of corn. When I went after her I knew not where she was, nor how far she had been chased that day; but, whether she was one or two miles distant, I always went that road where my mind led me, and constantly went as straight to her as I had actually known where she was, and never missed her track, but found her every night, the whole five weeks, whether she was east, west, north or south. And when I came I was entertained with an account of all the chasings her pursuers had given her, and how they had threatened to rob her of her corn. I told her Boaz was not in the field; if he had been, he would not have served her so. It is true we use his words in our church service, "The Lord be with you," and the pious reapers reply, "and with thy spirit," but this language is now quite out of fashion in our harvest fields.

Notwithstanding their chasing the clergyman's wife from field to field, she gleaned as much or more than Ruth of old did. As for our harvest, that was piled up on each side of our bed, which served instead of curtains. So we slept, defended with the staff of life, having all our tithes in our bed chamber (which, by the by, I believe was one of the smallest tithe-barns in Christendom). Our corn was threshed out in the chamber, and winnowed on the marsh, a sheet serving for a barn floor. The whole quantity of our wheat, when measured, amounted to four bushels and a quarter, exclusive of some peas and a little barley. My wife threshed out the corn and baked the bread, and I paid her so much per loaf as an encouragement to her future industry, and to buy her such necessaries as she wanted.

In the following winter the Lord sent a very deep snow, which lay a considerable time on the ground. Our wheat was now of great use to us, as it supplied us with bread for two or three months. But we were shortly brought into another strait through this snow. We used to buy fagots of our landlady to burn (being all the fuel we could get at that time), who one night informed us that she had but ten fagots left, which she must keep for herself, as there was no likelihood of the snow going away. Therefore she said she could sell us no more. To this I replied that, if she was in trouble for fear of suffering with the cold, when she had so much wood by her, surely we had much more cause to fear who had a young child. However, I begged of God that night to take away the snow, or send us something to burn, that our little one might not perish with the cold; and the next morning the snow was all gone. God had sent out his word and melted it, he had caused his wind to blow, and the water to flow (Ps. cxlvii. 18).

After some time our wheat was gone, and we were obliged to eat barley again; and, having paid away our money to redeem our clothes, we began to get very short of other necessary apparel, which, however, we soon retrieved; for, as I worked by day, cobbled at night, and lived upon barley, we kept ourselves out of debt, and tolerably decent in clothes. But this living on barley was attended with very bad consequences: for, as I had never been used to it before, and now living almost entirely upon it, without mixing it with wheat, it threw a violent humor into my eyes, and for some months I was in danger of losing my sight; but, by using one simple thing or other, they got better. My second daughter brought the same humor into the world with her, and both myself and the child had it, more or less, for some years, though not so violently as at first. I have often viewed this affliction on the child with great grief; but, in answer to prayer, God healed her eyes and mine too, so that our sight was perfectly recovered.

When harvest came on again we went to gleaning as before, and got no less than five bushels of corn; but my wife was pursued as formerly, for my continuing to preach had alarmed and much offended almost the whole parish, therefore they were more fierce in pursuing her. On the other hand, some were afraid of going near her, lest they should catch a religious infection; it being reported abroad that there was something of a power that seized upon them, and that, if we once got them to hear what we had to say, there was no getting away from our religion, as this secret something that seized them held them so fast that they must immediately change their own religion. I have known some men whom I have met go quite out of the path, and take a circle in the field, rather than pass me on the road; just as if that secret something could not seize them while walking on the grass as well as on the foot-path.

Chapter III.

I NOW BEGAN TO lose favor with my master; having preached among the poor people till some of them refused to work on the Lord's Day. Wherefore he inquired into the cause and was informed that the gardener had been preaching to them against profaning the Lord's Day, which was the reason why some would not work on that day. Others murmured because they were compelled to labor while some were exempted. This provoked him much, and he said he should expect me to work in the garden on the Lord's Day. I told him I did not choose to do that. He then swore at me, saying that, if I did not, I should not work for him. I replied that I would not, if I lost my employment; so, in a few days after, he told me, with several imprecations, to work no more for him. He owed me a trifle for a few days' work; but as he did not offer to pay me, I never asked him for it. I was informed that he expected me to come back with a suppliant knee; but I was determined that I would not sell my conscience for a loaf of barley bread, as it had cost my Savior so much to purge it; therefore I set off for Thames Ditton, and carried coals in the river for fourteen months at ten shillings per week, and preached during that time on the

Lord's Day, and one evening lecture in the week. All this time I suffered much both in body and mind, and found that the iniquity of those who wrought with me began to harden my heart; therefore I was determined to leave that situation, and go to my old business again. I got three or four day's work at Mousley, when a farmer came to my master, and told him to discharge me, having begun to preach out of doors. It was here that I committed this great offense of preaching Jesus Christ in the highway. On this account I was turned out of employment, and remained so for three weeks; during which time a gentleman at Mitcham sent for me to come over there the week following, to preach in their meeting, as he had long entertained a great desire of hearing me.

A few days before this a gentleman had given me an old black coat and waistcoat; which, being very large, made coat, waistcoat and breeches for me. So on the day appointed I put on my parsonic attire, which was the first time I ever appeared clad in that color, my usual appearance being more like the ploughman or the fisherman; but now I appeared in the external habit of a priest. And surely the good hand of my God was with me, and I went and delivered my message in his name. As it had been reported that a *coal-heaver* was coming to preach, there were a great many people gathered together to hear me. After I had finished my discourse, a lady came to me and gave me a new book, and blessed me; a gentleman, too, put a letter in my hand, laying an injunction upon me not to open it till I got home, in which I found enclosed a guinea and four shillings, with these words written: "Take this as from the hand of the Lord, for the laborer is worthy of his hire" (Luke x. 17).

These kind providences of God did wonderfully endear the Lord to me, and brought me to live by the faith of him for a supply of all my wants; and indeed I was obliged to do it, for I could get no employment. And, though I had preaching enough for a bishop, yet I had nothing coming in to live upon for so doing; my flocks were as poor as myself, at least the generality of them, and my family still continued increasing.

In this dilemma, a professor of the gospel, who was by trade a shoemaker, asked me one day to come to him and learn to make children's shoes; which at last I agreed to, and learned to make them (though in a very rough manner) in a short space of time.

I now took my work home to my house, and wrought there; and a few poor journeymen, who attended my ministry, and were single men (and therefore not so poor as their pastor), gave me some tools; till at length I became a shoemaker, and worked at it for my bread, while the love of Christ constrained me to preach for the good of souls, without making the gospel a burden to any. I was now in as bad a state as poor Paul, who preached the gospel freely, and made tents for his livelihood; his own hands ministering to his necessities, while his tongue was ministering to the necessities of thousands. If he had preached up heathen morality he need not have fared so hard, for the world loves that, and the preachers of it. The Savior says, "The world loves her own; and she never serves her own children as she does the children of God."

As I began this business so late in life, I was a very slow hand at it; and therefore was obliged to turn my *help-meet* into a *shop-mate,* that is, I taught my wife to close the shoes which I made; and both of us could earn about eight shillings per week. I had now five times a week to preach constantly; on which account I was forced to lay the Bible in a chair by me, and now and then read a little, in order to furnish myself with matter for the pulpit. It sometimes happened that I was under sore temptations and desertions; the Bible too appeared a sealed book, insomuch that I could not furnish myself with a text. Nor durst I leave my work in order to study or read the Bible;

if I did, my little ones would soon want bread. My business would also run very badly at those times. I therefore found the ministry of the gospel to be work enough for any man, without leaving the Word of God to serve tables.

After I had been about eight or ten months at this trade, my master failed in business, and nobody else would employ me. I was now a fortnight or more out of work, which sorely tried me indeed; for it so happened that we were forced to put our little ones to bed one night without supper, and their dinner was a very scanty one. When they saw me look in the cupboard, and shut the door again without giving them any thing, they lisped out some very pathetic, though broken accents, expressive of want, which touched my parental feelings very sorely, and took away my rest for that night. In the morning I got up and went out, but where to go I knew not. I could not endure the thought of staying at home to see my little ones want bread. But these words were sweet and suitable to me: "He hath chosen the poor of this world, rich in faith and heirs of the kingdom." And I well knew it was "easier for a camel to go through the needle's eye than for a rich man to enter the kingdom of God." In this miserable situation I knew not where to go. If I left off preaching, and run from the work (as Jonah did), I should deny the Lord that bought me. Though I was willing to work, yet none would employ me on account of my religion; and if I stayed at home my little ones were crying for bread. Indeed, I should often have run from the work of God, had not his terrors stood on my conscience in battle array against me. At this time no book could suit me but the Lamentations of Jeremiah. To these I constantly fled for comfort; for, like him, I often was for running away, but could not; therefore God fulfilled his word, "They shall be my people, and shall not depart from me." I went that morning as far as Kingston, but where I was to find relief I knew not; however, just as I came into the town, it suddenly came in my mind to go to Mr. Chapman, then living on Hounslow-Heath, a person who had known me for some years, even before either of us knew the Lord, and who was called by grace about the same time that I was. He had often invited me to come and visit him, wherefore I now obeyed the impulse which I felt, and accordingly went over Kingston bridge directly to Hounslow-Heath, where I found him and his wife at home. I was, however, determined not to make my deep distress known to them, but intended to watch the good hand of my God in this journey. The good man and his wife received me very affectionately; and, after kindly entertaining me, loaded me home with many simple dainties for the children, though at that time they knew not how I had left them. And it came to pass, when I departed, that the good man walked two miles with me, and on the road offered me a guinea, which I refused, saying that, if he would give me half a guinea, I would accept it, provided it was with his wife's knowledge. He said it was. So I took the half-guinea, wondering how I should pay for the fare of the bridge to get home, fearing they might not be able to give me change, but I cast my eyes on the ground, and there lay a penny, which served to pay the toll of the bridge. So I got home safe, and was received with a hearty welcome. And thus I made a better voyage of it than Naomi, who went out full and returned empty.

As I had lost all my employment in shoemaking, I was obliged to try another branch of business. I therefore commenced *cobbling*. But as none would employ me in this business except those who attended my ministry, sometimes I had work and sometimes I had none. So that I found this branch of business attended with many inconveniences, for it often happened at the beginning of the week that I had a little to do, and at the latter end rather more than I could get done; which, with sitting up till twelve o'clock in the Saturday night, and having eleven miles to walk, and three times to preach on the Lord's day, rendered my labors too hard for me, as my living was very inconsiderable. However, God made this circumstance of great use to my soul, therefore it was one of the all-things that work together for good.

I had naturally a very great flow of spirits, so that this poor way of living gradually brought on me an inward weakness, attended with the loss of appetite, which rendered me incapable of taking that nourishment my labors necessarily required. I could drink nothing but water or small beer for some years together, which at times brought me so low that I was obliged to gird my stomach with a handkerchief as tight as I could bear it, in order to gather strength to enable me to deliver three discourses a day. At length I got so low that one pint of good small beer rendered me incapable of walking steady; and Satan violently tempted me on this head. Some of my friends, who saw the case I was in, fearing that I should shortly come to an end, labored hard to dissuade me from this mode of living, but in vain. Sometimes they would mix my small beer with a little ale, which I could immediately detect, and was apt to view them my enemies for so doing; but they did it through fear that I should throw myself into a consumption, and that one little branch of the church of Christ might thereby sustain a loss. For five years I went on in this manner, till there was scarce one step between me and death. But I gradually got rid of this habit, as the Lord appeared more precious to me in a way of providence, and God sanctified it to the good of my soul; for this poverty and bad living brought many infirmities on me, which have at times lain as a canker-worm at the root of my natural levity. I now began clearly to see that God intended to establish me as a preacher of the gospel, by his opening many doors for me, and because many souls were awakened by my instrumentality. Blessed be God, such shall be my joy and crown of rejoicing in the day of the Lord Jesus.

I found it, however, impossible to preach five or six times a week, and carry on the business of cobbling at the same time; especially as it generally came in so fast at the latter end of the week, a time when I wanted to study the Scriptures, in order to furnish myself with matter for the Lord's day. Wherefore I determined to give up this employment, and continue in the work of God only, whatever I might suffer by it. In consequence of this resolution, I went to a poor cobbler, who lived in the same place with me, and to him I gave my kit of tools, threw myself entirely on the propitious arm of kind Providence, and gave myself wholly to the ministry of the Word and prayer.

At this time I had left my ready-furnished lodgings, and rented a little cottage at three pounds eighteen shillings per annum; and we had about half as much furniture to put in it as a porter would carry at one load.

Having thus left off my cobbling business, Providence exercised my faith and patience very sharply at times, and suffered me to get a little behind-hand in the world, which caused me to cry and pray day and night, for I knew that the cause in which I had embarked would be exposed to contempt if I contracted a debt and could not pay it. And though this is not felt by the rich, yet it lies heavy on the mind of the poor, honest Christian. But in answer to prayer, God sent to my house a gentleman of great property, very much noted in the religious world for liberality, who, after he had stayed with me a few hours, ordered his carriage, and at his departure gave me five guineas, at which I was amazed, he being a stranger to me, and one whom I had never before seen. This served to buy me some few household necessaries, as also to pay off the debt which I had contracted. Oh, who would not choose the precious life of dependency on God, when the tender regard of Providence in our poverty is so clearly seen in those rich supplies which are poured forth in answer to the simple, though powerful, prayer of faith!

At this time I stood in great need of linen, and of a new suit of clothes, my old black ones being almost worn out. I often begged this favor of God, agreeable to his own word. "If God so clothe the grass, which to-day is, and to-morrow is cast into the oven, will he not much more clothe you, O ye of little faith?" But God exercised my patience long, teaching me the necessity of importunity in prayer, and at last answered me by terrible things in righteousness; for he sent a violent storm of persecution, which, from its proving intolerable, obliged me to seek redress from the law of the land, as I was legally licensed. My appeal, however, proved in vain; for, upon the trial, my license proved an improper one, from the word *teacher*, or *preacher*, being left out of it, which was not my fault, as I had applied and procured it legally. I was now obliged to go to London and get another license. And here the answer to my former prayers appeared. I was obliged to tarry in town all night, and, as there was a person who had long wanted to see me (not from any personal knowledge of me, but from various reports he had heard of the Lord's dealings with me), I endeavored to find him out, and accordingly did. He received me very courteously, and kindly entertained me, at a time of my undergoing a sharp trial. "A man's own heart deviseth his way, but the Lord directeth his steps."

As answers to prayer now seemed to be wholly denied, my faith in God's providence began to fail. And in very deed I was determined to leave my ministerial work, and go and settle at Guilford, where I thought I could get employed as a gardener, and preach to my little flock at Wooking on the Lord's Day. But alas! "there are many devices in a man's heart, but the counsel of the Lord that shall stand." However, in order to accomplish this with some degree of conscience, I endeavored to get a supply of ministers for the various places I preached at. But all my efforts were in vain. And indeed there was little encouragement for any to undertake to supply them, as they were so distant from London, and as it was in much opposition that the cause was carried on; besides, there were neither tithes, offerings, nor surplice fees attending their labors. Those who undertook the work must have gone on this warfare entirely at their own expense.

As I could not possibly get any assistance in my ministerial labors, I knew not how to go on, having no clothes fit to be seen in. I suffered, too, even for want of the common necessaries of life, for I had as much traveling and preaching as I was able to do, had I lived ever so well; but being obliged to live very low, I was hardly able to go through the work in any shape. I was as bad off as poor Paul: I suffered hunger, cold and nakedness.

The good man whom I have before mentioned, and at whose house I lodged that night, purposed that I should go into Sussex, to preach at the place of his nativity. I told him that the apparel I then had on was all the clothes I was possessed of, wherefore I was really not fit to be seen anywhere, and that I was likewise in debt. He asked me if I would stay and preach in one of his rooms in the evening to a few friends he would invite. I complied with his request, and accordingly preached, where three gentlemen gave me each a guinea. The good man also went to some of his friends, and made up the sum to nine guineas, with which I got proper clothing and other necessaries; and there was a little money left to pay some debts which I had contracted. Thus I went home with a full answer to my prayers, and in my second suit of parsonic attire. This circumstance much encouraged my faith in

God's providence, and caused me perpetually to beg of God to be my only provider, teacher and master; and that he would always direct my steps and supply my wants, and not leave me dependent on an arm of flesh. In my prayers I often made this my plea: that, as he had called me without the instrumentality of any preacher, and sent me out without the approbation or disapprobation of any one, and had in a way of providence opened many doors before me, and blessed my labors to the good of many souls; he would also let his providence appear to me as I might stand in need of it — that I might not be burdened with cares about what I should eat or what I should drink, or wherewithal I should be clothed; but that I might devote body, soul, time and talents to the glory of his name, and to the good of his chosen. These petitions God has been pleased to answer in some measure ever since. "I have been young, and now am old; yet have not seen the righteous forsaken, nor his seed begging bread."

At my return from London, I could not help making my boast of God, even in the pulpit. And, as my persecutors had burnt me in effigy a little while before, I told my audience that God had sent me a new suit of clothes as it were out of the ashes, my persecutors having burnt a suit, with which they clothed the effigy, not much unlike my old one. Seeing me thus clad was a great grief to the opposers of God; they were sorry to see any raised up to seek the welfare of the children of Israel.

I had now a pleasing gale of prosperity for some time, but shortly after another cloud of frowning providences gathered thick over my head, and kept me long in suspense, until I had run fourteen or fifteen pounds in debt; more by ten pounds than I had ever owed before. But, as my faith in Providence had been sharply tried, and was strengthened by these trials, a greater burden was laid upon me. And thus I found faith's task to be always proportionable to her strength. In the midst of this trouble, the little flock at Wooking desired me to take the charge of, and to be ordained over them, to which I consented, and gave my promise. On my return home afterwards, however, Satan violently tempted me, and unbelief and carnal reason fell in with the temptation. It was for having refused some calls in the country, where the people would have supported me as their pastor if I would have accepted their call; but now, as I had agreed to take the charge of a flock that could not support me, I should be for ever tied down from accepting any other call, that my family was still increasing, that I was deeply in debt, that my clothes were got as bad as ever, that my year was now out, and that my gracious master had not given me a new livery, nor was there any appearance of it. But, blessed be God, I had the inward recompense of a good conscience, because I did not take the oversight of God's flock for filthy lucre, but of a ready mind.

Having waded some time in this dreadful flood, I began at length to reason, from past experience, that God had hitherto been gracious; and, as *he* had set me to work, I must look to him for my wages. But this Satan attempted to overthrow, by suggesting that I was never so much in debt before. Which I knew to be true, so that my faith began to fail, and I mistrusted the providence of God. But these words came so sweet to my mind, and with so much power, that they bore down all that the tempter could suggest, "Seek ye first the kingdom of God and his righteousness, and all these things will be added unto you." "A word spoken in due season is like apples of gold in pictures of silver."

The next day, in the evening, I preached at Hammersmith; and when I came down from the pulpit a gentleman desired me to call at his house, where he had ordered a tailor to measure me for a suit of clothes, of which he intended to make me a present. As soon as the words were out of his mouth the same Scripture recoiled with power on my mind, "Seek ye the kingdom of God and his righteousness, and all these things shall be added unto you." I hung down my head and wept for joy at the goodness of my God to one who was so slow of heart to believe. In a few days my clothes were made, and I went and received them. This was one sharp blow to my unbelief, and led me to see that God took care to order apparel for me as well as for Aaron and his sons.

Now the principle and most difficult work of faith was to reconcile my mind as to the discharge of my large debt. And how this was to be done I knew not; but this I knew, that I had not imprudently presumed on God's providence, having contracted it merely to supply my wants; and, as the Lord made me trust him for the fulfillment of his promises, I was forced to get others to trust me till my faith could get her wages in. That I scored up my blessed Master, who, in his own time, always discharged my debts with honor. Thus God, who wrought a miracle to clear the debt of a poor widow by Elisha the prophet, will surely clear the just debts of his ministers.

Chapter IV.

Soon after this my friend in London asked me, and I agreed, to preach at his house; and on the day appointed I went, when he told me that he had consulted the managers of Margaret Street Chapel about my preaching there, to which they had agreed; and it was advertised that I should preach there that night. At this I was sorely offended, being very much averse to preaching in London, for several reasons. First, because I had been told it abounded so much with all sorts of errors that I was afraid of falling into them, there were so many that lay in wait to deceive. Secondly, because I had no learning, and therefore feared I should not be able to deliver myself with any degree of propriety; and as I knew nothing of Greek or Hebrew, nor even of English grammar, that I should be exposed to the scourging tongue of every critic in London. However, I preached that night, and soon after found myself induced, by sundry persuasions, to preach the word of God statedly in that very chapel. During many weeks I labored under much distress of mind, respecting my want of abilities to preach in this great metropolis. But God in due time removed that distress by condescending to bless his word, even from my mouth, and he was pleased to deliver a young man from a capital error by the first discourse I ever delivered at that place, which appeared not only a great encouragement to me at that time, but also a prelude to that future success which I might expect under God's promised blessing. The above mentioned young man is now a preacher of the gospel, and has been instrumental in calling others. So that I am become a grandfather from my first London discourse.

Being a native of the Wild of Kent, which is none of the most polite parts of the world, I retained a good deal of my provincial dialect, and many of my expressions, to the ears of a grammarian, sounded very harsh and uncouth. This circumstance caused many unsanctified critics to laugh and cavil at me. But, when God permitted me to drop promiscuously into company with any of those who were so very learned, and they began to pour contempt on some of my expressions, I generally found them very deficient in the work of the Spirit on their own souls; and though some of them seemed very wise in gospel doctrines, yet I could easily find that their knowledge was borrowed from commentators, by their appearing great strangers to the experience of them on their hearts, and also to the happy enjoyment of them, which I knew they would be able to give account of, if they had received them wet with dew and warm with love from heaven, in answer to the prayer of faith. It is true that some have often confounded me in the sense and meaning of words, as also in the original texts, yet I found that I could as much confound them in the sensible operations of the Holy Ghost, agreeable to the word of God; and, by my own experience of the Spirit's work, could overthrow some expressions of theirs from the Hebrew language, especially those who labored to overthrow the divinity of the Son of God; the manifestation of whom to my own soul, agreeable to his word, has enabled me to foil the most accomplished Arian I have ever yet contended with upon that point. The only way to prove Christ's divinity is to go to him when overwhelmed with guilt and horror, and to pray to him as the eternal God; and, if he appear to honor our faith and to answer our prayers, and deliver us from the wrath of God, the guilt of sin, the power of Satan, the fear of death, the curse of the law, and eternal damnation, and blesses us with pardon, peace, love and liberty, he shall be the eternal God of our soul's salvation, though Satan be the god of this unhallowed world. For, though the Arians talk of Christ as a *stone of help*, yet, if they allow him to be no more than a creature, they might as well call him a *sandy foundation* as a *rock*; for all flesh is dust, and to dust it must return. If he had not been God, he certainly would have seen corruption, as well as other creatures have done; and that he was raised from the dead is not owing to his being man, but to his being God—"put to death in the flesh, but quickened by the Spirit." His flesh was raised without seeing corruption, because he was the Son of God with power, and had immortality and eternal life in himself, as the self-existent and independent Jehovah. And God the Father prepared a body for him, and he willingly came and took it on him to do his Father's will, so he wore that fleshly garment till he had finished the work his Father gave him to do, and then dipped it in blood, and sanctified himself for our sakes, that he might sanctify us; he then laid it down for our life, and raised it again for our justification; took it at last to heaven as the first fruits of them that sleep, and appears in it as in an eternal temple, wherein dwells the glorious Shekinah, or "all the fullness of the Godhead bodily." All our access to God is only through that rent vail of his flesh; and he who allows Christ to be no more than a creature, denies all the intrinsic glory of the eternal Godhead that ever dwelt between the cherubims, and condemns every hoping soul that ever took shelter under the shadowing wings of the Almighty.

Upon the whole, I found my ignorance of Greek and Hebrew to be no impediment in the way of the Spirit of power, as I firmly believed that God had written his law on my heart; and I am persuaded that what the Holy Ghost writes on the mind of man is always agreeable to the original text, and that, if there are any errors in our English translation, the blessed Spirit will never impress the minds of God's elect from a false copy, nor appear as the broad seal of heaven to ratify a lie. No; "he shall guide you into all truth, and he shall glorify me."

But I shall now return to my former subject, and inform my reader how my faith managed the great debt before mentioned, God having long exercised my faith and patience, until I began to despair of ever getting it paid. It so happened that a capital error crept into the church of God at Horsham in Sussex; and some friends sent for me, as it was a place where I had often preached. Indeed it was the first place that I ever preached at in a public manner. I therefore complied with their request, and in my way thither was blessed with one of the most comfortable and lively frames of mind that I had ever enjoyed. This frame was attended with a most delightful chain of heavenly meditations, which, when I arrived at my journey's end, I committed to paper, and sent a friend in town. This circumstance, under God, paved a way for my being invited to preach at Chelsea, where I delivered a discourse from the text: "Children, have ye any meat?" I was afterward informed that a confirmed Arian came out of curiosity to hear me, and, though I knew nothing of it, I was led in the course of my sermon to be very severe against the destructive tenets of the sect, in consequence of which he went home convinced; and upon his arrival there was seized with a fit of illness, during which Christ was graciously pleased to manifest his atonement to his conscience. When he felt the power, he cried out, "The darkness is now past, and the true light shineth." He continued in this divine ecstasy till his body dropped into the jaws of death, which was about a fortnight after the above discourse was delivered. Thus God fulfills his word, "Those that erred in spirit shall come to understanding, and those that murmured shall learn doctrine."

But to return to my subject. A gentleman, famous for a liberal turn of mind, asked me to lodge at his house, with which I gladly complied; and in the evening he inquired about my health, ministerial success, and also concerning my circumstances. As God alone knew my wants, so none but God could have inclined his heart to relieve me. At my departure he gave me ten guineas. This precious answer to prayer, coming so seasonably in time of need, put my discontent to the blush, dashed infidelity itself out of countenance, and stopped the mouth of an accusing devil. "Trust in the Lord, and do good; so shalt thou dwell in the land, and verily thou shalt be fed" (Ps. xxxvii. 3).

I found God's promises to be the Christian's bank note; and a living faith will always draw on the divine Banker; yea, and the spirit of prayer, and a deep sense of want, will give an heir of promise a filial boldness at the inexhaustible bank of heaven.

Indeed the providence of God is a great mystery; nor could I unriddle it, even while I was daily exercised with it. During my residence at Ewell I have often begun the week with eighteen or twenty pence, sometimes with two shillings, and sometimes with half a crown; and we have lived through the whole week upon that only, without contracting any debt. And I found it impossible at the week's end, upon the best reflection I could make, to tell how we have been supported through the week. At other times I have found that my craving appetite had lost its keenness, insomuch that I have been able to work hard for two days together without any food at all. And sometimes God has indulged me with such heavenly views of a glorified state, and entertained my mind with such sweet contemplations on futurity, that my dinner hour has passed away unnoticed; nor have I once had a thought about it till four or five o'clock, nor near the time of leaving my labor. But these blessed acts of God's providential regard are nothing new; for he took away the appetite of Moses and Elijah for forty days together; and he is the same God still. Nor is his bountiful hand at all shortened, though the faith of the necessitous has so often stretched it out. "I will leave in the midst of thee a poor and an afflicted people, and they shall trust in the name of the Lord" (Zeph. iii. 12).

At my return I discharged my debt as far as the ten guineas would go, and left the other standing on the book, which Providence used as a future exercise for my faith. About that time I was ordained over my little flock at Wooking; when I found Providence began to frown again, in order to keep me humble. However, all things worked together for my good; for, being kept daily dependent on God's providence by faith, I had the precious enjoyment of sweet communion with God; and every day did his providence and gracious care appear more or less over me. I generally found those blessings the sweetest which had caused me the most importunity in prayer. This makes the "dinner of herbs, where love is, better than a stalled ox and hatred therewith" (Prov. xv. 17).

Some time after this I was brought into another strait, by receiving a letter that required me to give up one of my little flocks, which happened to be at that time my chief support. This plot was laid by a person who made a god of his wealth, and therefore found fault with my sermons, conceiving them levelled at him. And indeed the allegation was certainly well founded; for, if a man has got the world in his heart, the preacher is sure of hitting him, if he should only draw a bow at a venture, for, if the love of money be the root of all evil, it is impossible to wield the sword of the Spirit without cutting either root or branch.

This treatment drove me to London. When I left my own home on the Lord's day morning, my whole stock of money amounted to no more than two pence, of which I took one half and left my wife with the other. One half penny of this I paid at Hampton Court bridge; and soon after a poor man asked alms of me, to whom I gave the other half penny. Then I besought the Lord not to send any other person to ask alms of me, until his bountiful hand had supplied my own wants. However, this trial also worked together for my good; for it was the means of bringing me to preach constantly in London; and many who had heard me in town, met with me at my friend's house, and invited me to preach at Margaret Street Chapel. Several friends also sent for me to their houses. One gave me a guinea, and others half a guinea, till I had enough to discharge the debt I owed.

Mentioning these minute circumstances has offended many; and some (of an independent fortune) have condemned my prayers as carnal, in praying for such temporal things; but I know that they have taken many worse steps both to accumulate and to keep their independence. I think it is better to beg than to steal, as say those who speak in proverbs.

I now wanted to return home, fearing that my family would want bread; but just before the time of my departure, a friend from Richmond arrived, who informed me that he had been to Ditton, and supplied the wants of my family; for he said he had been informed of the affair, and guessed how my pocket stood. "Oh, that men would praise the Lord for his goodness, and for his wonderful

CHAPTER 4 | 49

works to the children of men!" "Go thy way, eat thy bread with joy, and drink thy wine with a merry heart; for God now accepteth thy works" (Eccl. ix. 7).

At my return home I discharged my debts, and for a time went sweetly on, under the sunshine both of Providence and grace; and God sent me back again to the flock which I had been commanded to leave by the mouth of a rich and covetous professor. Thus God frustrates the counsels of the wicked, so that his hands cannot perform his enterprise.

But, as the life of faith consists in bearing the cross of Christ, we must not expect to be long without trials. Providence soon frowned on me again, and I got behindhand as usual. This happened, too, at a time when my wife was sick, and destitute of those necessaries of life which are needful at such times. The nurse came and told her there was no tea in the house. My wife replied, "Set the kettle on, if there is not." The nurse (whose name was Ann Webb, a daughter of mine in the faith, and the first soul that God called by me) said, "You have no tea, nor can you get any." My wife replied, "Set the kettle." She did so; and before it boiled, a woman (with whom at that time we had no acquaintance) came to the door, and told the nurse that she had brought some tea as a present to my wife. Thus God, who showed Moses a stick to sweeten the waters of Marah, sent a little tea to bitter the water in my wife's kettle. Soon after my wife recovered, tidings were brought to us that a gospel minister was coming down to Kingston to preach an evening lecture, and to break bread to the congregation. I had a great desire to go to the table, and also to have my child baptized at the same time; but, as I never could go from the Lord's table without offering my mite, and at this time had no money in my pocket, I could not go. However, I begged of God to send me a little money some way or other for this purpose; which I verily believed he would. So I waited till within half an hour of the time to go, and then began to think I should be disappointed; but, just as unbelief set me to murmuring and complaining, I heard a man ride up to my door as I was in my study at the back part of the house; and when he rode away again I called to my wife to get ready to go. "Get ready!" said she, "why you know we have no money!" "Poh! Poh!" said I, "God has sent money!"

And true enough it was that God had sent it; for all the business the man had with us was to give us some money! Surely it was God that sent him, and none else; for, if the hairs of our heads are all numbered, we have reason to believe that our wants are; and if God keeps our hairs from falling to the ground, he certainly supplies our wants too. Thus the good God and Saviour, who made a fish produce money for an earthly tribute, sent the man with three shillings as an offering to God, and of his own we offered to him (I Chron. xxix. 14).

Soon after this I was obliged to borrow a guinea of a certain friend, which I promised to pay him on the Thursday night following, if he would call for it. And I begged of God to send it me from some quarter or other, firmly believing he would. The day before my friend had appointed to call on me for the money, I was to go out to preach among my friends; and I earnestly besought God to send it me that day, if it was his will and pleasure, of which I had no more doubt than of my own existence. However, I returned home without it, and wondered how it could be, seeing the Saviour says, "Whatsoever ye shall ask, believing, ye shall have it; and nothing shall be impossible unto you." I told the Lord that I had prayed in faith for it, firmly believing that I should have it, but had not obtained it. This text of scripture came with power to my mind, "Faith is the substance of things hoped for, and the evidence of things not seen." I had from that time a sweet view of that passage, and delivered several discourses from it which God seemed to bless with power. But to return to my subject. As soon as I came home I began to fret because I had not the money that I expected; but still the text answered me, "Faith is the substance of things hoped for," etc. I replied, "If it be the *substance,* it is as sure as the thing itself." Upon this the good man came into my study, and I was going to make an apology to him; but before I opened my mouth, he said, "I came to desire you not to think of paying me the guinea, for I have made you a present of it, and God bless you with it." As soon as he was gone the same passage of scripture recoiled upon my mind again with much comfort, "Faith is the substance of things hoped for," etc. And indeed I clearly saw it to be so, both in spirituals and temporals. Thus my faith was not confounded, nor my hope disappointed; all my trouble sprung from my own sin, which was limiting the Holy One of Israel. I was expecting money to pay the debt, but God took away from my creditor the expectation of payment. Thus, like Joseph's brethren, I intended to show myself faithful and honest, by paying the money; but our spiritual Joseph was minded to show me that he had given me treasure in the heart of my creditor.

About that time a person called upon me, and offered to let me the house he then lived in, which he was going to leave. I own I had a desire after it, because there was a large garden belonging to it, which I could look after myself, and raise many vegetables, that would help to support my family. The garden was walled in, too, which I much admired, being very fond of retirement. There was a stable, a brew-house, and every other convenience; and the rent was only six pounds ten shillings per annum. But the man told me it would cost seven or eight pounds to take the fixtures of the house; wherefore I gave up the thoughts of it, as I had no view of raising such a sum. So I drove it from my thoughts, though I much wanted it. But God hath "determined the times before appointed, and the bounds of our habitations; that we should seek the Lord" (Acts xvii. 26).

A few days after this a friend called to see me; whom I consulted about the house, and showed it to him. He persuaded me to take it, which I accordingly did, but was obliged to wait a few weeks, till the person I was to succeed could provide himself with another situation suitable for his business. I therefore asked God in prayer to enable me to purchase the fixtures of this house, if it was agreeable to his sovereign will and pleasure; for I knew that God had "set the bounds of the people according to the number of the children of Israel" (Deut. xxxii. 8). And the providence of God appeared so conspicuous, that I shortly obtained money enough to pay for the fixtures; but the person desired me to wait a few weeks longer, as he had been disappointed of the house he expected to go into; so I waited two months, during which time the money was all spent. Then I begged of God to frustrate my going into the house at all, if it was displeasing to him, although I much wanted it; because my little cot was placed in a very vulgar neighborhood, and the windows were so very low that I could not study at any of them without being exposed to the view of my enemies, who often threw stones through the glass, or saluted me with a volley of oaths or imprecations. This was very disagreeable to me. In my public ministrations I expected nothing else but the cruel venom of asps; but to commune with my God in private was the only sweet refuge I had to flee to, and the only door of hope that was open for comfort and relief. However, Providence soon began to shine again; and indeed I had nothing else to live on from year's end to year's end but what God sent me in answer to prayer. At this time a person gave me five guineas; which kind providence I rather wondered at. But, the following night I had a dream—I hope my brethren will not hate me yet the more because of my dreams (Gen. xxxvii 5), seeing we have a scriptural warrant for the relation of them: "He that hath a dream, let him tell a dream; and he that hath my word, let him speak my word" (Jer. xxiii. 28),—I dreamed that the person before mentioned sent to inform me that he was going to leave his house; that the things were to be appraised on Friday morning; and that he should expect me to pay him the money down for the fixtures. I said in my dream, "Lord, thou knowest I cannot go, for I have not money enough." Then came this answer, "Go to Mr. Munday, cutler, at Kingston upon Thames, and he will lend you as much as you want." I soon after awoke, and behold it was a dream! therefore I took little notice of it. But in a few hours the person sent me word that he was going to leave his house, and should expect me to come and see the things appraised the next morning, and pay him the same. Then I began to think that it was more than a dream. The same night, Mr. Munday, of Kingston, called on me; and to the best of my remembrance he had never been at my house before. I asked him if he would lend me a little money. He replied, "I will lend you all I have in my pocket; and, if you will call on me to-morrow at Kingston, I will lend you five pounds if you want it." He accordingly lent me what he then had with him; and the next morning, after the things were appraised to me, I paid for them, having just nine shillings left. This is the end of my dream. Whether this blessing came from Fortune on the wheel, or from the Searcher and Disposer of hearts, I shall leave those to determine who have got learning and independent fortune at command.

Chapter V.

MY YEAR BEING NOW expired, I wanted a new parsonic livery; wherefore in humble prayer I told my most blessed Lord and Master that my year was out and my apparel bad; that I had nowhere to go for these things but to him, and as he had promised to give his servants food and raiment, I hoped he would fulfill his promise to me, though one of the worst of them. Seeing no immediate signs of my livery coming, I began to omit praying for it, though God says, "For all these things I will be inquired of by the house of Israel, that I may do these things for them." It fell out one day that I called on a poor man, who complained that he could not attend the word of God for want of apparel. This drove me to pray again for my new suit of clothes, that I might give my old ones to him. A few days after this I was desired to call at a gentleman's house near London. Indeed it had been impressed on my mind for six weeks before that God would use that gentleman as an instrument to furnish me with my next suit. And so it fell out; for, when I called on him, upon leaving his house he went a little way with me, and while we were on the road he said, "I think you want a suit of clothes." I answered, "Yes, sir, I do; and I know a poor man that would be very glad of this which I have on, if my Master would furnish me with another." When we parted he desired me to call on him the next morning, which I accordingly did, when he sent a tailor into the room, and generously told me to be measured for what clothes I chose, and a great coat also. When I got the new, I furnished the poor man with my old suit. This was the fourth suit of apparel that my Master gave me in this providential manner, in answer to the prayer of faith. This God, who kept Israel's clothes from waxing old, though in constant use for forty years, gave me a new suit every year.

I was soon afterwards brought into another strait. Having contracted a debt of five pounds for some necessaries which I wanted, I promised to pay it on a certain day; and I put up many prayers that God would enable me to fulfill my promise. At last the day arrived, and I had not one farthing towards it. About ten o'clock the bell rung at my gate. Supposing it to be my creditor, I kneeled down, and begged of God not to let him come till he had sent me that money to pay him. It proved not to be the man I expected, but soon after the bell rung again, and I kneeled down again, and prayed with the same words, and was informed a stranger wanted to see me. He had much to say to me about the things of God, and when he left me he gave me two guineas. Soon after this I went to work in my garden, and another person, who lived at a great distance, came to speak with me, and gave me another guinea. After that I took a walk in the fields, and met with two gentlemen who feared God, and who came from London on purpose to see me. They gave me two guineas. The next day my creditor came, and his money was ready for him. This is like the Lord's dealings with the poor widow by Elisha, when the creditor came to take the mother and son for bond-servants, God sent the creditor all his demands in a pot of oil.

I have omitted one providence which has just occurred to my mind, and which happened at the time I carried coals for my bread. It fell out one night that we were forced to put our little ones to bed without a supper, which grieved me much, and on which account I got but little sleep all night, for I lay and wept bitterly all night under my hard fate. While I was weeping and praying a person came to the window and told me there was a load of wooden hoops come to the wharf from Dorking, in Surrey, and that I must get up and unload them, which I soon did. When I had done, the farmer told me he had brought me a little meat pie and a flagon of cider, of which he had heard me say I was very fond. As soon as he was gone I went home and endeavored to awake my young ones, but in vain; however, I set them up on the bolster, and they began to eat before they were fully awake. Thus God sent food from a very remote place in answer to the groaning petition of my burdened heart.

God grant that, if my reader be a poor Christian, he may take encouragement from these accounts to pray and watch the hand of God in every time of trouble, until he sees, agreeable to the promise, that God causes all his goodness to pass before him. Oh, how sweet is the least mercy when fitly timed, and brought forth so seasonably! how it endears God to the soul! When the poor widow of Zarepta was gathering two sticks to bake the last cake for her and her son, that they might eat once more before they died, then comes the man of God, and swears that the barrel of meal shall not fail till God send rain upon the earth (I Kings xvii. 14).

At this time I had many doors opened to me for preaching the gospel, very wide apart. I preached at Margaret street in London, at Richmond, at Ditton, at Cobham, at

Wooking, at Worplesdon, and at Farnham, in Surrey. This I found too much for my strength. However, I continued for a considerable time, till at last I was generally laid up sick about once a month. I found I had great need of a horse, but feared I should not be able to keep it if I had one. However, it happened that I had a very severe week's work to do; I was to go to Wooking and preach on the Lord's Day morning, to Worplesdon in the afternoon, and from thence to Farnham in the evening; to preach at Petworth, in Sussex, on the Monday, at Horsham on the Tuesday, at Margaret street chapel on the Wednesday, and at Ditton on the Thursday evening; but before I could reach Ditton on the Wednesday I was so far spent that I thought I must have lain down on the road; yet with much difficulty I reached home, and then I had to go to London. Finding myself wholly unable to perform all this labor, I went to prayer, and besought God to give me more strength, less work, or a horse. I used my *prayers* as gunners use their swivels, turning them every way as the various cases required. I then hired a horse to ride to town; and, when I came there, went to put him up at Mr. Jackson's livery stables, near the chapel, in Margaret street, but the ostler told me they had not room to take him in. I asked if his master was in the yard. He said yes. I desired to see him, and he told me he could not take the horse in. I was then going out of the yard, when he stepped after me, and asked if I was the person that preached at Margaret street chapel. I told him I was. He burst into tears, saying he would send one of his own horses out and take mine in; and informed me of his coming one night to hear me out of curiosity, because he had been informed that I had been a coal-heaver. He then told me that, under the first sermon, God showed him the insufficiency of his own wretched righteousness, the carnality and hypocrisy of his religion, the true state of his soul, and the necessity of the spirit and grace of Christ Jesus the Lord to change his heart if ever he was saved; and blessed God for sending me there. This was good news to me. He also said that some of my friends had been gathering money to buy me a horse, and that he gave something towards him. Directly after I found the horse was bought and paid for; and one person gave me a guinea to buy a bridle, another gave me two whips, a third gave me something necessary for the stable, another trusted me for a saddle, and here was a full answer to my prayer. So I mounted my horse and rode home; and he turned out as good an animal as ever was rode. I believe this horse was the gift of God, because he tells me in his Word that all the beasts of the forest are his, and so are the cattle on a thousand hills. I have often thought that, if my horse could have spoken, he would have had more to say than Balaam's ass; as he might have said, "I am an answer to my master's prayers; I live by my master's faith, travel with mysteries, and suffer persecution, but I do not know for what," for many a stone has been thrown at him.

On my road home, while meditating on the manifold blessings I had received from God, both in a way of grace and providence, how unworthy I was of them, and how unthankful I had been for them, I told God that I had more work for my faith now than heretofore; for the horse would cost half as much to keep him as my whole family. In answer to which this scripture came to my mind with power and comfort, "Dwell in the land and do good, and verily thou shalt be fed." This was a bank note put into the hand of my faith; which, when I got poor, I pleaded before God, and he answered it. So that I lived and cleared my way just as well when I had my horse to keep as I did before; for I could not then get anything either to eat, drink, wear, or use, without begging it of God. Sometimes I found much murmuring in my heart against being held in so tight a rein; for which I was sure to suffer afterwards. So I found, by daily experience, that I could not add one cubit to God's stature, no, not even in the least thing; therefore it was in vain for me to take thought for the rest.

Having now had my horse for some time, and riding a great deal every week, I soon wore my *breeches* out, as they were not fit to ride in. I hope the reader will excuse my mentioning the word *breeches*, which I should have avoided, had not this passage of scripture obtruded into my mind just as I had resolved in my own thoughts not to mention this kind providence of God, "And thou shalt make them linen breeches to cover their nakedness; from the loins even unto the thighs shall they reach. And they shall be upon Aaron and upon his sons when they come into the tabernacle of the congregation, or when they come near unto the altar to minister in the holy place; that they bear not iniquity and die. It shall be a statute forever unto him and his seed after him" (Exo. xxviii. 42, 43) By which, and three others (namely, Ezek. xliv. 18; Lev. Vi. 10; and Levi. xvi. 4), I saw that it was no crime to mention the word *breeches*, nor the way in which God sent them to me, — Aaron and his sons being clothed entirely by Providence, and as God himself condescended to give orders what they should be made of, and how they should be cut. And I believe that the same God ordered mine, as I trust it will appear in the following history.

The scripture tells us to call no man master, for one is our master, even Christ. I therefore told my most bountiful and ever-adored Master what I wanted; and he, who stripped Adam and Eve of their fig-leaved aprons, and made coats of skin and clothed them, and who clothes the grass of the field, which to-day is and to-morrow is cast into the oven, must clothe us, or we shall soon go naked; and so Israel found it, when God took away his wool and his flax, which he gave to cover their nakedness, and which they prepared for Baal, for which iniquity was their skirts discovered, and their heels made bare (Jer. xiii. 22).

I often made very free in my prayers with my invaluable Master for this favor; but he still kept me so amazingly poor that I could not get them at any rate. At last I was determined to go to a friend of mine at Kingston, who is of that branch of business, to bespeak a pair, and to get him to trust me until my Master sent me money to pay him. I was that day going to London, fully determined to engage them as I rode through the town. However, when I passed the shop, I forgot it. When I came to London I called on Mr. Croucher, a shoemaker in Shepherd's Market, who told me a parcel was left there for me, but what it was he knew not. I opened it, and behold there was a pair of *leather breeches* with a note in them! the substance of which was, to the best of my remembrance, as follows:

"Sɪʀ:

"I have sent you a pair of breeches, and hope they will fit. I beg you acceptance of them; and, if they want any alteration, leave in a note what the alteration is, and I will call in a few days and alter them.   I.S."

I tried them on, and they fitted as well as if I had been measured for them, at which I was amazed, having never been measured by any leather breeches maker in London. I wrote an answer to the note to this effect:

"Sɪʀ:

"I received your present, and thank you for it. I was going to order a pair of leather breeches to be made, because I did not know till now that my Master had bespoke them of you. They fit very well, which fully convinces me that the same God who moved thy heart to give, guided thy hand to cut; because he perfectly knows my size, having clothed me in a miraculous manner for near five years. When you are in trouble, sir, I hope you will tell my Master of this, and what you have done for me, and he will repay you with honor."

That is as near as I am able to relate it, and I added:

"I cannot make out *I. S.* unless I put *I* for *Israelite indeed,* and *S.* for *Sincerity,* because you did not "sound a trumpet before you, as the hypocrites do."

About this time twelve-month I got another pair of breeches in the same extraordinary manner, without my ever being measured for them.

As I was one frosty night going to Richmond to preach, when there was much snow on the ground, I met a poor cripple in a very deplorable condition. He solicited alms of me, and I refused him, because I had but one shilling in all the world, and did not choose to part with that; however, I found myself greatly distressed because I did not give it to him, he appeared in such a miserable condition. I thought, perhaps, in such a severe night as that was, he might perish for want of the necessaries of life. When I came to Richmond I told a friend of it, and said I thought him to be in a dreadful situation, because I was so much distressed about refusing to relieve him; declaring that if I met him again, I would give it to him, if I never had another shilling of my own. The next night, as I was going to preach at a village adjacent, I met the same poor object, and had got the same shilling in my pocket, and no more. The poor creature passed me, but asked nothing of me; however, I turned back and gave him the shilling. The poor man received it with great joy and thankfulness, and told me a deal of his sufferings, which fully convinced me he was in great want; and this blessed passage of Scripture came to my mind: "He that hath pity upon the poor lendeth to the Lord; and that which he hath given will he pay him again" (Prov. xix. 17). I went that night and delivered my discourse, and when I had done a woman took me aside into a room, and put three half-crown pieces into my hand, saying, "I was commanded to give you that." I asked her, "By whom?" She replied, "By a gentleman; but you are not to know his name." Thus I received my shilling again with very considerable interest; and thus also the fulfillment of the word took place: "There is that scattereth and yet increaseth; and there is that withholdeth more than is meet, and it tendeth to penury" (Prov. xi. 24).

One providence I had almost forgot. We were at that time very badly off for beds and bedding; my children were no better provided than the Saviour when he lay in a manger, for they slept upon bags of hay; but prayer at a long run brought in these things also. Some of my most intimate acquaintances knew how I was tried in this respect, though I never made it known to anybody who was capable of helping me out of my trouble. But one night, after I had done preaching at Richmond, a person invited me home to his house, and showed me a large bundle tied up, saying it was for me. I asked who the donor was; he replied, "You are not to know that." I carried it home, when lo, it proved to be bedding, and the very thing I stood so much in need of! Thus the blessed Saviour fulfills his gracious promise which he made to his servants, "Whatsoever ye ask in my name, that will I do, that the Father may be glorified in the Son. If ye shall ask any thing in my name, I will do it" (John xiv. 13, 14).

Some time after this I took gospel courage and asked my Master to give me a new bed; and importuned his ever-blessed and most excellent Majesty until I got it. Perceiving that the Lord approved of a bold, though not of presumptuous beggar, agreeable to his word, "Let us come boldly unto the throne of grace," etc., I boldly asked him the favor, and persevered in it, until I was one day informed by a friend that four or five pious people were coming on such a day from London to visit me. Then my faith told me that I should soon have the bed. Accordingly they came, and we had some comfortable conversation together. Towards evening they departed, giving me four guineas. Oh, what Christian in his right mind would murmur and complain at his poverty, when, with a watchful eye, he sees such liberal supplies poured forth from the inexhaustible stores of Providence! Thus God, who provided a comfortable lodging for Elisha the prophet, provided me "a bed, a table, a stool and a candlestick" (2 Kings iv. 10).

I was determined to keep this money for a bed, and therefore went to a good man in London and bespoke one, which he very soon sent me, with a rug also, and a pair of very good blankets. Soon after I called to pay him for it, when he told me to pay his clerk, who gave me a receipt for the same; but afterwards the gentleman went a little way with me, and at his departure gave me all the money back again. How sweet are temporal mercies when received by those who are under the influence of grace! when they are seen to come from a covenant God and Father, in answer to the simple prayer of faith! Surely he that "will observe these things, even he shall understand the loving kindness of the Lord" (Ps. cvii. 43). The promises of God pleaded in humble prayer, and promised mercies received in answer thereto, always come so as to make a divine impression, being sweetened with love to us; for every such mercy is "sanctified by the word of God and prayer." But to the unbelieving and prayerless there is nothing clean, though there be ever so much stock in hand. "A little that a righteous man hath is better than the treasures of many wicked" (Ps. xxxvi. 16).

Chapter VI.

ANOTHER YEAR HAVING ROLLED over my head, I began to look about for my livery; for I always took care to let my most propitious Master know when my year was out. And indeed I wanted it bad enough, for riding on horseback soiled my clothes much more than walking did. However, my Lord exercised my faith and patience for six weeks together about this livery, and I looked all manner of ways for it; but every door seemed shut up; and I could not see from what quarter it was to come. (You know, reader, we are *all* very fond of running before God; but he takes his own pace.) At length I was informed by Mr. Byrchmore that a gentleman in Wells Street wanted to see me. Accordingly I went; and was admitted into the parlor to the gentleman and his spouse. He wept, and begged I would not be angry at what he was going to relate; which was, that he had for some time desired to make me a present of a suit of clothes, but was afraid that I should be offended at his offer, and refuse it. "Ah!" says Envy, "there need be no fear of that, for Methodist parsons are all for what they can get." It is true; for we are commanded to "covet earnestly the best things," and so we do, and expect a double reward of the Lord,— one in this world, the other in the next. And this is no more than our Master has promised to give us; for we are to "receive an hundred-fold in this world, and in the world to come, life everlasting." I told the good man that I had been for some time expecting a suit of clothes, but knew not how to procure them. They both wept for joy upon my accepting them, and I wept for joy that they gave them so freely. As they had been fearful that I should be offended at their offer, and not receive them; so I had been much exercised in my mind, lest my Master would not give them to me, as he usually had done. However, our minds were now eased of our fears, on both sides, and I was clothed; and it was the best suit that I ever had. This is the fifth livery that my trembling hand of faith put on my back, and every one came from a different quarter. The name of the good man who gave me this suit is Randall, in Wells Street, Oxford market. I mention his name to show that I cannot keep such secrets, because he strictly charged me not to let it be known. However, I have imitated the disciples of old in this, for it is said of them that "the more Christ charged them to keep silence, the more they spread it abroad." And indeed it must be so, or else the Lord would be deprived of the honor that is due to his holy name. Though by the Saviour's charge it plainly appeared that he sought not the applause of men, yet it is the indispensable duty of every Christian to applaud the Saviour.

But to return to my subject. I had an invitation to go and preach at Horsham, in Sussex, one Monday evening. On the preceding Lord's day I preached at Wooking, in Surrey, and had to ride from thence to Horsham on the Monday. Then I set out to go across the country (it was in the winter season); and just as I had got out of Guildford town it began to rain, and continued in a violent manner all the time I was on the road. It so happened that I had but one shilling in my pocket, which would only procure a feed of corn for my horse, and pay the turnpikes. My surtout, which was a very thin Bath coat, was of very little use, being almost worn out; wherefore I was much exposed to this violent storm of rain, and I think I never had been so wet before. I was obliged to strip, and even to have my shirt washed before I could preach. I then secretly wished for a large horseman's coat, being obliged to ride in all weathers; but, as I had been begging so many things of my most indulgent Master, I thought by my continual coming I should weary him, not considering that God commands us to open our mouths wide that he may fill them, which I believe means that our desires should be as extensive at a throne of grace as God's pregnant promises, which he made us in the dear Son of his love. Christ is the heir of all things, and the Christian is an heir of promise, therefore he has a right to ask for those things that will defray his expenses through this world with that honor which becomes a saint, and not a miser.

My mock-modesty would not allow me to ask God for a great coat, though I earnestly desired it, and murmured at God's providence because I was kept so poor that I could not purchase one. However, when I came to London on the Wednesday following, and had preached at Margaret Street Chapel in the evening, a person approached me just as I came out of the chapel, saying, "I want to speak to you;" which was to inform me that he intended, with assistance of some more friends, to make me a present of a horseman's coat, wherefore he desired me to be measured for it. Accordingly I was, and that gentleman, with a few others, honorably paid for it. Surely to deny the overruling providence of God is to deny the whole journal of the children of Israel, and all the wondrous works of God which daily appeared on their behalf for forty years together. But there are some who consider not "the operation of God's hands; therefore he shall destroy them, and not build them up" (Ps. xxviii. 5).

Thus my mock-modesty could not make the promise of God of none effect; and God forbid it ever should. Zechariah desired a sign when the angel told him that his prayer was heard, and a son was to be given; and God gave him an awful sign, but his unbelief did not hinder the birth of John. After receiving this gift from God this scripture came sweet to my soul: "I know both how to be abased, and I know how to abound; everywhere and in all things I am instructed both to be full and to be hungry, both to abound and to suffer need" (Phil. iv. 12). And indeed I found by all these trials that I also was instructed, for I learned one blessed doctrine by this providence, which I never saw clearly before; namely, the power of internal or mental prayer ascending so prevalently to God, under the influences of the Spirit, even when the understanding and the lips were both unfruitful. And the application of the following texts gave me sweet views of it: "Lord, thou hast heard the desire of the humble: thou wilt prepare their heart, thou wilt cause thine ear to hear" (Ps. x. 17). "Delight thyself also in the Lord, and he shall give thee the desire of thine heart." "Commit thy ways unto the Lord; trust also in him and he shall bring it to pass" (Ps. xxxvii. 4, 5). These scriptures led me to consider, and apply with comfort to my own soul, the many precious promises which God has made in Christ Jesus to the spiritual anxiety of a renewed soul at the throne of grace, even when the sound of the voice, the sound of the organ, and that confused gabbling of monkish mimicry, called chanting of prayers, are left quite out of the promise; as will appear in the following passages, which I beseech my reader to consider: "The desire of the righteous shall be granted" (Prov. x. 24). "For he satisfieth the longing soul, and filleth the hungry soul with goodness" (Ps. cvii. 9). "For the oppression of the poor, for the sighing of the needy, now will I arise, saith the Lord; I will set him in safety from him that puffeth at him"; "For he looked down from the height of his sanctuary; from heaven did the Lord behold the earth; to hear the groaning of the prisoner (mark that, to hear the groaning of the prisoner); to loose those that are appointed to death" (Ps. cii. 19, 20). Thus the Holy Ghost makes "intercession for the saints according to the will of God; and God, who searcheth the heart, knoweth what is the mind of the Spirit" (Rom. viii. 27).

Hence observe, reader, that the promise is made to a spiritual hunger, a spiritual thirst, an holy longing, a deep heart-felt sigh, an earnest desire, and groaning, from a burdened mind. All these are petitions put up by the blessed Spirit of supplication alone (without the use of the lips), who "maketh intercession for us with groaning that cannot be uttered." These were the prayers which our blessed Saviour put up at Lazarus's grave, "when he groaned in the spirit, and was troubled." "Jesus therefore again groaned" in spirit. (John xi. 33, 38). Again, "And Jesus looking up to heaven, sighed, and saith unto him, Ephphatha; that is, Be opened. And straightway his ears were opened, and the string of his tongue was loosed, and he spake plain" (Mark vii. 34, 35). Thus it appears that agonies, tears, groans and sighs, were chiefly the all-prevailing petitions put up by our dear Redeemer when in a state of humiliation. Christian, learn thou of him who is meek and lowly in heart, and thou shalt find rest for thy soul.

It is not an eloquent voice, elegant speech, lofty compliments, swelling words, much speaking, long prayers, nor yet the numberless repetitions of "We beseech thee to hear us, good Lord," that shall ever prevail with God; it is "not every one that saith, Lord, Lord, shall enter into the kingdom." The foolish virgins were too late with Lord,

Lord. God will accept of no sacrifice but that which comes in the hallowed flame of his own kindling, and perfumed with sweet-smelling savor of that blessed, ever-availing, and ever-living sacrifice of his dear Son. The prayers of that man who calls himself a Christian, or a follower of the Saviour, but is an utter stranger to *mental* prayer, have never yet reached the ears of God; for God is a spirit, and will accept of nothing short of spiritual prayer. It was the groanings of the children of Israel that went up before God, and brought him down to deliver them, as declared by God himself to Moses at Horeb (Ex. ii. 24). Let this encourage thee, reader, if thou art one who cannot find words to express thyself at the throne of grace. If thou canst pour out thy soul before the Lord, show him thy trouble, and leave thy burden with him. These are precious prayers; and, if thou comest from thy knees with thy mind eased, thy faith strengthened, thy hope encouraged, thy bowels refreshed, and with confidence that God hath heard thy prayer for his dear Son's sake, oh, these are sweet answers from God. Be thankful, and pray on. Such was the answer that Hannah got when she went from Shiloh with her countenance no more sad.

During the space of three years I secretly wished in my soul that God would favor me with a chapel of my own, being sick of the errors that were perpetually broached by some one or other in Margaret street chapel, where I then preached. But, though I so much desired this, yet I could not ask God for such a favor, thinking it was not to be brought about by one so very mean, low and poor as myself. However, God sent a person, unknown to me, to look at a certain spot, who afterward took me to look at it; but I trembled at the very though of such an immense undertaking. Then God stirred up a wise man to offer to build a chapel, and to manage the whole work without fee or reward. God drew the pattern on his imagination while he was hearing me preach a sermon. I then took the ground, this person executed the plan; and the chapel sprung up like a mushroom. As soon as it was finished this precious Scripture came sweet to my soul: "He will fulfill the desire of them that fear him" (Psalms cxlv. 19). Thus the chapel appeared as an answer to the earnest desire which God had kindled in my heart, and which he intended to fulfill in his own good time, to the honor of his own great name, the good of many souls, and to the encouragement of my poor, weak, tottering faith. It is confessed in the Church of England service that "all holy desires, all good counsels and just works, proceed from God," and I believe they do.

Another kind providence I experienced while I resided at Thames Ditton. My surtout coat had got very thin and bad, and the weather at that time was very cold. It happened that I was invited to preach at a little place near London. As I went thither I felt the cold very severely; and as soon as I had delivered my discourse, I desired a young man to fetch my old great coat, in order to put it on before I went out of the warm meeting-house. When he came back, lo, he brought me a *new* one! I told him that was not mine. He said it was. And though I insisted upon it that it was not, he persisted in saying it was. So I put it on and it fitted me very well. In one of the pockets there was a letter, which informed me that my blessed Lord and Master had sent it to me to wrap my poor worthless carcass in during that very severe winter. Oh, the tender care of our most gracious Lord and Master! Solomon says, "The favor of a king is as a cloud of the latter rain." I think he must mean the cloud of God's divine favor, which blotted out our transgressions as a cloud, and appears as a cloud by day to screen us from the storm of wrath; and, if my reader watches the bountiful hand of God, he will see this blessed cloud daily discharging itself in the genial showers of grace and providence; as it is written, "And I will make them, and the places round about my hill, a blessing; and I will cause the shower to come down in his season, there shall be showers of blessings" (Ezek. xxxiv. 26).

They have a common saying in the Wild of Kent when the daughter of an old farmer is married. If it be inquired what portion the old man gave, the answer is, "He gave not much money, but the old people are always sending them something, — there is always something sent from a farm-house." Then the observation usually is, "Ay, hers is a hand-basket portion, which is generally the best, for there is no end to that." Even so our everlasting Father gives to his poor children a hand-basket portion, — a basket being that which we generally fetch our daily provisions in. God sometimes puts his blessing even in a basket, and then it seldom comes home empty; as it is written, "Blessed shall be thy basket" (Deut. xxviii. 5). Our blessed Saviour eyed this promise on the mount. When he was going to feed five thousand men, besides women and children, with five barley loaves and two small fishes, it is said he looked up to heaven, and blessed and brake, etc. And that blessing was enough; for they were all filled, and there were twelve baskets full of fragments. Thus the blessings appeared in the basket; and that made the Saviour so fond of the fragments as to give this strict charge to his disciples, "Let nothing be lost." Thus, too, the proverb of the hand-basket portion appears true; and our blessed Saviour himself lived on it while he dwelt below, yea, the whole Levitical tribe lived on the hand-basket portion, for the shew-bread, that was set hot before God on the golden table, was brought in a basket. So that God himself has highly honored the basket.

I am firmly of opinion that the hand-basket portion is the best, both for soul and body; because it keeps us to prayer, exercises our faith, engages our watchfulness, and excites to gratitude. It does not appear that the prodigal son added much to his fortune when he desired the portion of goods that fell to him; that is, desired to have an independent stock of his own, and to be left to improve it by himself; wherefore he did not choose to live near his father, lest he should interfere; but went into a far country, that his father might see how he flourished in the world when once he became independent. But self-will, self-sufficiency, and independency of God, seldom gain much by trading, for we all know that this independent merchant would have been starved, and damned too, if free grace had not undertook to feed him and to save him. Poor soul! I warrant you he flourished away at first, but he soon brought himself down upon a level with the swine. He could not boast of the *entertainment,* because it was nothing but *husks;* nor could he boast much of *company,* they being only *swine.*

Chapter VII.

I ONCE PREACHED ON the Lord's Day at Wooking, in Surrey; and the week before that time I and my family had been sorely tried for want of the common necessaries of life. I was very fond of feeding my little ones when I had wherewithal to feed them, because I knew how much I had suffered when young through my parents' poverty. That week the little ones had lived chiefly on bread, which grieved me much, as the appetite of young growing children is so craving after food. When I used to shut the cupboard door, and give them nothing but bread, my eldest daughter would look me in the face with much earnestness and solemnity, and ask me this important question, "Is the boo *all* boppee, daddy?" which gibberish, by interpretation, signified, "Is the butter all gone, father?" She would at such times lean her head on one shoulder, look me full in the face, and lay a particular emphasis upon the particle *all,* which she would draw out with a very long tone. Then she would use some of her logic, and reason the point with me, asking me many strange questions, which I partly understood, as they amounted chiefly to the inquiry when the butter would come, or whether there was any ground to hope for any; but at that time I could give her no promise as a ground for her hope, every door being apparently shut.

We had at that season but little fuel, though it was a very severe frost and the snow laid on the ground. As I was returning from Wooking on the Monday morning, before I came to Cobham (having left Wooking very early without breakfast), I was exceedingly hungry and weary, and had but little to expect when I arrived at home; for I knew I had nothing but bread, and perhaps not that. When I came on the common which is called Fair Mile, lying between Cobham and Esher, I wept bitterly at my hard fate, and yet trembled for fear of offending God by my complaining, as he had given me so full a persuasion of my eternal salvation through Christ. I often feared that he would hear my murmurings as he did the murmuring of Israel in the wilderness, when he answered them by terrible things, namely "He gave them meat for their lust, but sent leanness into their souls." And I thought, if God should take away the happy enjoyment of his love from me and lay me in a stock of temporal things instead thereof, I should have cause, like Job, to curse the day wherein the change was made; therefore I often prayed against that, and the blessed Spirit greatly helped my infirmities in those prayers.

But when I got about half over the common, it came suddenly into my mind to go out of the horse road into a little narrow track, which leads over the hills, between the hand-post and the Bath-house. I could gain but very little ground by this, nor do I remember that I had ever gone that way before; but I soon found what this impression meant; for there was to be a battle fought between a stoat, or weasel, and a large rabbit. The stoat, or weasel, was to fight the battle and to win the field, and I was to take the prey. So I took up my rabbit and gladly carried him home, and it proved as fine a one as I ever saw, being quite in the season, in every sense of the word, for we had nothing but bread in the house.

I endeavored as much as possible to get my wife to live by faith; and often encouraged her to prayer, by telling her that she had a right to expect her support from God as well as myself, seeing the Almighty had taken me from my daily labor to work in his vineyard; and I supported my argument from this consideration, that the whole Levitical tribe lived of old on the offerings of the Lord, both women and children, as well as those men who waited at the altar.

Soon after this Providence sent me three guineas, with which I was determined to furnish my wife with some apparel. I accordingly bought her a gown and soon after a friend gave her another. At this she seemed highly pleased. Her unbelief was confounded, her murmuring stopped, and all was well. After this the bountiful hand of my Lord seemed to be closed again for a long time; until I got five guineas in debt, and began to want even provisions. Now I began to fret, and unbelief crept in apace; but, just as the spirit of murmuring and complaining began to operate, there came a letter to me from a gentleman at Gainsborough in Lincolnshire. I opened it and found the following contents:

"DEAR FRIEND, — I have sent you a hamper by one of my ships, which will be at London by such a time, if God permit; and I have ordered it to be left at Hungerford-Stairs for you. The first present is for your wife, which is *two ends*; the other is for your children, being *a cow and her milk-maid attending her*—a cow being very useful where there is a family; the last article, according to my judgment, is a very useful thing for you, and for every gospel minister.

Tender my best respects to your wife and little ones, and accept the same from

"Your humble servant,

"J. D."

Here is the riddle, and I had seven days to find it out. My wife asked me if my present was a Bible. I said no, I believed not. I told her that Paul called a gospel minister an ox. "Thou shalt not muzzle the mouth of the ox that treadeth out the corn. Doth God take care of oxen, or saith he it altogether for our sakes? For our sakes no doubt this is written." "Thus," said I, "God compares a preacher to an ox. Treading out the corn is unfolding and explaining God's word; muzzling the ox is not giving him food to eat for his labor, as Paul explains it. 'Even so hath the Lord ordained, that they which preach the gospel should live of the gospel'" (I Cor. ix. 14). I farther added that the same apostle, who compares the preacher to an ox, tells us in his epistle to the church at Colosse, to "let our speech be always with grace, seasoned with salt, that we may know how we ought to answer every man" (Col. iv. 6). Therefore I conjectured that my present was a *bullock's tongue, well salted;* and that my wife's, which the letter expressed to be *two ends,* must be *a flitch of bacon, cut into two pieces;* but, as for a cow I could not conjecture what that could be. When the hamper came, we all got round it, to see what was the substance of the riddle in the carcass of the lion; and when it was opened, I found that my present was a *bullock's tongue dried;* my wife's was *two large pieces of bacon;* and the children's present was a *cheese, with the print of a cow and milk-maid milking her on it.* Such was the present, and this was the explanation of the riddle.

About this time I went once a fortnight to preach at a place in Middlesex, about ten miles from London where I lived, and they gave me three shillings a time for preaching to them. There was a single gentleman, who was a member of the church, a man of great property, supposed to be with twenty or thirty thousand pounds. This gentleman once saw me pass by his door, as I had been that way to visit a sick woman. He called me into his house, and expressed much love to my Master, Jesus, and a great satisfaction in hearing my discourses on the doctrine of grace; and desired me, the next time I came, to deliver a discourse from this passage of scripture: "But the land whither ye go to possess it, is the land of hills and valleys, and drinketh water of the rain of heaven; a land which the Lord thy God careth for; the eyes of the Lord thy God are upon it, from the beginning of the year even unto the end of the year" (Deut. xi. 11, 12). So I promised to offer my thoughts on the text when I came again to preach. At my departure he gave me the right-hand of fellowship, blessed me in the name of the Lord, and, putting his hand into his pocket, very generously made me a present of *a whole shilling!* I took it, and thanked him kindly; for I thought it was the first fruits of liberality that ever grew upon that tree, and perhaps that last; and I mention it now to the honor of his compassionate bowels. I afterward found that he made many inquiries concerning me; and had been informed that I was a poor man; had a large family; that I walked ten miles out and ten miles back again, and was from home all night when I preached at that place, for which I received only three shillings. These things reaching his ears, conveyed that sympathetic touch to his feelings, and finally dragged that *whole shilling* out of his pericardium. "How hardly shall those that have riches enter the kingdom of God!"

I believe that every man has a god of some sort or other. *Self* is the god of the Pharisee; the *belly* the god of the epicurean; *mammon* the god of the miser; and *Jehovah* the God of the Christian. And all these have their representatives. Hager is the mother of the Pharisees; Nabal the head of the gluttons; Judas of the mammonites; and Simon Magus is the figurative sire of every person who is laboring hard to purchase the grace of God, and the gifts of the Holy Ghost, by their own supposed merit.

Having been one night to preach at Richmond, I was invited home by my friends, Mr. and Mrs. Chapman, at Petersham, near Richmond, to sleep. In the morning Mrs. Chapman, smiling, told me she had twelve yards of stuff damask by her, which she intended to make me a present of, for a morning gown. I laughed, and told them that I thought a coal-heaver would cut a strange figure in a morning gown. I should appear like a beggar in dignity; but that was better than dignity in ruins. However, they saw that God had begun to lift up my head, and were determined their pastor should make a more respectable figure; wherefore they insisted on my having it; to which I objected, because a gown has such a cottish appearance on a laborer in the vineyard. I therefore turned it into a banyan, or coat; and after it was made up I hid it for two or three months before I could reconcile myself to appear in it.

I had now received a letter from a friend in the country, who was in great distress, and stood much in need of a little relief; but at that time I myself was four or five pounds in debt, which I had been a long time in expectation that my God would enable me to discharge. However, I found that God now began to try my patience; and that I ought to importune, and watch, and wait upon the Lord, and to keep my eye fixed on him, as a servant's eye is on the hand of his master, and until I obtained an answer. And I never waited on his blessed Majesty in vain, for it was sure to come at length. After putting up my petitions, and having been kept long in suspense, I one night called on Mr. and Mrs. Smith, in Chandler Street, Oxford road, who were great friends to me. Before I departed they generously made me a present of three guineas. I humbly beg their pardon for mentioning their names, and exposing their secret alms; but, as I prayed to my Father which seeth in secret, and he in mercy rewarded me openly, I therefore must proclaim it upon the house-top, to encourage the weak faith of others, that they may make God their Guardian and their Bank. The liberality of Job's friends is left upon record to their honor, when "every man gave him a piece of money, and every one an ear-ring of gold (Job xlii. 11).

I now took encouragement to hope that my gracious Master would add to this blessing a sufficiency for the purpose of discharging my debt, and relieving my friend; which, in answer to prayer, he was graciously pleased to do. The next morning a person knocked at my door, desiring to see me. When he came into my study I looked at him, and perceived him to be a gentleman that I had never seen before. He told me that he had once heard me preach at Dr. Gifford's meeting house, and once or twice in Margaret Street Chapel, and that he had heard me greatly to his satisfaction; and the reason of his coming to see me now was, that he had been exercised the last night with a dream — that he dreamed that the word of God came to him saying, "If thy brother be waxed poor, thou shalt open thy hand to the poor brother," etc. He asked me if there was such a portion of scripture. I answered the words were these: "If there be among you a poor man, one of thy brethren, within any of thy gates, in the land which the Lord thy God giveth thee, thou shalt not harden thy heart, nor shut thine hand from thy poor brother; but thou shalt open thine hand wide unto him, and shall surely lend him sufficient for his need, in that which he wanteth. Beware that there be not a thought in thy wicked heart, saying, the seventh year, the year of release, is at hand; and thine eye be evil against thy poor brother, and thou givest him nought, and he cry unto the Lord against thee, and it be sin unto thee. Thou shalt

surely give him, and thine heart shall not be grieved when
thou givest him; because that for this thing the Lord thy
God shall bless thee in all thy works, and in all that thou
puttest thine hand unto. For the poor shall never cease
out of the land. Wherefore I command thee, saying, Thou
shalt open thine hand wide unto thy brother, to thy poor,
and to thy needy in the land" (Deut. xv. 7-11). He told
me many of these words came to him in his sleep; and in
the morning, when he awoke, he felt the power of them.
In wondering who this poor brother could be, he informed
me it was impressed on his mind that I was the brother
about whom he had dreamed; and asked me concerning
my circumstances. I then told him of the trial I was in;
and, as he was fully satisfied it was of God, he wondered
much at it. At his departure he gave me a new pair of
dogskin gloves, two new white handkerchiefs, very good,
and a guinea. He then blessed me, and left me; and I do
not remember ever seeing him before that time, nor but
once since. Thus God who commanded a widow to sustain Elijah, commanded this man to relieve me.

The next day a friend told me that a person had left a
guinea with him for me; and, while at Mr. Byrchmore's
in Margaret street, a lady came to his door in a coach,
inquiring for me. When I came to the door, she put her
hand out and gave me a guinea, and then ordered the
coachman to drive away, having done all the business
God sent her to do. Thus our most bountiful Benefactor
answered these my poor petitions also, after he had been
pleased for a time to exercise my faith and patience, in
order to encourage me to a stronger confidence in his
grace and providence. And I now make it known to the
honor of his veracity, and to the encouragement of the
poor of his flock, who are obliged to live, both spiritually
and temporally, "by every word that proceedeth out of
the mouth of God." And, as God has been pleased to reveal himself as a God that will hear and answer prayer,

and has appeared so to *me,* one of the worst and least of all creatures, I choose therefore to subscribe with my hands (Isa. xliv. 5); set to my seal; and proclaim to all that fear his name, that God is true (John iii. 33).

Oh, how sweet have these words often been to my soul! and as applicable to my case as possible: "And thou shalt remember all the ways which the Lord thy God led thee these forty years in the wilderness, to humble thee and to prove thee, to know what was in thine heart, whether thou wouldest keep his commandments or no. And he humbled thee, and suffered thee to hunger, and fed thee with manna, which thou knewest not, neither did thy fathers know; that he might make thee know that man doth not live by bread alone, but by every word that proceedeth out of the mouth of the Lord doth man live" (Deut. viii. 2, 3). When these precious answers to prayer appeared, they always came attended with humbling grace, and were sweetened to my soul with a blessed sense of unmerited love; and, though at certain times, when unbelief was prevalent, I have found it hard work to keep from murmuring; especially when I have seen the basest of mortals rolling in wealth and pleasure, and spending it to support the shattered interest of the devil; while I could appeal to God that I loved him, and sought his glory, and the good of his chosen, yea, even labored beyond my strength in his cause and interests and yet suffered for want of common necessaries. But these two scriptures generally silenced murmuring: "The wicked have their portion in this life, whose belly God fills with his hid treasure;" and "The righteous are God's witnesses against the wicked." These words would sometimes occur to my mind: "He that hath a bountiful eye shall be blessed." And again, "To one it is given to gather together and heap up, but never an heart given to do good therewith; this is a sore travail," And that in Job, "Though the wicked prepare raiment as the sand, yet the righteous shall put it on, and the innocent shall divide the silver." Better is the gospel contentment with poverty than the sacrifices of many wicked; and I have often found the most comfort in my soul when my outward matters have appeared to wear the most gloomy aspect—internal consolations have more than once counterbalanced all my external afflictions. These daily crosses attending me in circumstances I found were made very useful to those whom God had called by me, as the means to establish them in the faith of Christ, who is the Saviour of the body as well as the soul, and in whom the invaluable promise is yea and amen to every soul that is interested in his finished salvation. God hath given us all things in Christ, whether life or death; yea, we have the promise of the life that now is, and of that which is to come; which promise even includes "all things pertaining to life and godliness." Happy is that soul that credits God's promise; places his confidence in him for the fulfillment of it; makes use of the means God has appointed; daily pleads his promise in the humble prayer of faith; patiently waits his time; daily watches his hand; lives in a holy expectation of a daily supply of spiritual and temporal mercies from the God of his salvation; and who is humbly thankful to God for every favor that flows through the atoning blood and prevalent intercession of a dear Redeemer! I say, let not such envy the crowned head nor sceptred hand; for, if there be any virtue, or if there be any praise, if there be any serenity of mind, if any peace of conscience, if any honor to God, if any fruit brought forth to the glory of the Most High, it is to be found in such a soul; and he, with the greatest propriety, may be said to think on these things.

Chapter VIII.

WHEN PROVIDENCE HAD BEEN exercising my faith and patience till the cupboard was quite empty, in answer to simple prayer he sent one of the largest hams that I ever saw. Indeed, I saw clearly that I had nothing to do but to pray, to study, and to preach; for God took care of me, and my family also, agreeable to his own promise, "Seek ye first the kingdom of God and his righteousness, and all these things shall be added unto you." And I have often thought the reason why our dear Lord and Master gave no inheritance to the Levitical tribe, who performed the sanctuary service, was, that they might learn to live by faith, and likewise to exercise and try the liberality of the worshipping tribes. And this appears to be the reason why the apostles were sent out to preach without purse or scrip. Certainly God could have sent them out as rich as the sanhedrim had he thought proper. But no; he left the blind priest to live off the offerings and tithes of the blind followers, as their portion; and it is to be feared that was the only portion that some of them ever had from God. But the poor apostles were to go out with only a portion of grace in their hearts; and where they sowed those spiritual things, God opened the hearts of the converts to bring forth temporal things to them. And it often appeared that as soon as the grace of God had taken the government of a young convert's heart, his temporal riches appeared at the apostle's feet. Thus the gospel defrayed the expenses of the dispensers of it. And this I believe was intended to try the sincerity of the grace of those who were enabled to believe the gospel; as Paul put some of his followers upon a like trial, and made liberality one of the touchstones. "See that ye come not behind in this grace also." Yea, and even our dear Lord and Master lived on the alms of his followers; for, as soon as he was born, the Eastern sages opened their treasures, and presented unto him gold, frankincense, and myrrh; and even until his crucifixion he lived on the liberality of his poor disciples, who were said to minister to him of their substance. It is true, Satan offered him all the kingdoms of the world, and the glory of them, upon certain conditions; but he refused, choosing to suffer hunger rather than turn stones into bread to prove his Sonship, and please an accusing devil.

Providence was pleased again to try me, till I run five guineas in debt. After I had prayed and waited some time, a gentleman belonging to the Stamp-office (a very faithful friend to me for many years together, during my state of extreme poverty), called upon me, and generously made me a present of five guineas, which paid off that debt. Oh, the goodness of God to those that fear his name and hope in his mercy! He even sent a raven to feed the prophet Elijah, when he dwelt by the brook Cherith; an angel, too, was sent from heaven to bake him a cake on a fire, and bring him a cruse of water, when, being weary, he slept under the juniper tree, in his road to Horeb. "Arise and eat," said the celestial guest, "for the journey is too great for thee" (I Kings xix. 7).

I now began to get quite weary of living at Thames Ditton, as I did not see that God had anything more for me to do there. His word had appeared a savor of life unto life to some few, and a savor of death unto death to many, who were indefatigable in opposing it. In short, I secretly longed to leave it, but was determined not to do so until I saw the Lord himself open the door; for "when he puts forth his own sheep, he goes before them." I was fully persuaded that I should end my ministry in London, and had long told a friend in town of it. Another reason for my wanting to quit Ditton was the bad state of health that I felt myself in, which rendered me incapable of such long journeys and so much labor. But I have generally found God to kindle a desire in my heart after that which he intended to bring to pass. Thus, when the time came for Israel to leave Egypt, the spirit of supplication was sent to make intercession in many of their hearts, after their deliverance from bondage; and God told Moses he had heard the groanings of his people Israel, by reason of their task-masters; and "I am come down," said God, "to deliver them." And so it will appear even in this matter when I have related it.

After preaching at Wooking one evening, I returned home about twelve o'clock at night; and before I could shift myself and take care of my horse, it was between one and two. Having an infant very ill, I told my wife that I would lie alone that night, as the child was so very restless I was apprehensive I should get no rest myself, being very weary; and, having another journey to go the next day, I was fearful I should not be able to perform it unless I had some rest. Accordingly I went into another bed, and fell into a very sound sleep, when I dreamed; and behold, in my dream, I thought I heard the Lord call to me with a very shrill, distinct voice, saying, "Son of man! son of man, prophesy! Son of man, prophesy!" I answered, "Lord, what shall I prophesy?" The voice came again, saying, "Prophesy upon the thick boughs." I immediately awoke, and felt a comfortable power on my heart, and thought the voice seemed fresh in my ears. I knew not what it meant, nor did I remember ever seeing such words as "thick boughs" in the Bible. However, I got up immediately and traced my Bible, to see if I could find those words there; thinking that, if I could, I should conclude the dream to be from God. I soon found the words, and perceived the thick boughs to be men (Ezek. xxxi. 3; xvii. 23). But what the command could mean, I could not then tell, because I was employed in prophesying on the boughs almost every day. I went into my wife's room and told her of it, but observed at the same time that I could not think what it meant, though I should certainly know hereafter. The next day I came to London, and told it to Mr. Byrchmore, adding that I knew there was a mystery in it, and that, as it was from God, it would shortly be revealed to me. "God speaketh once, yea, twice, but man perceiveth it not; in a dream, in a vision of the night, when deep sleep falleth upon men, in slumbering upon the bed; then he openeth the ears of men, and sealeth their instruction" (Job xxxiii. 14, 15).

However, it passed on for some days entirely hid from me what the meaning could be. But I knew the vision would speak in time; and, though it tarried some days, yet I waited for it (Hab. ii. 3). I likewise told Mr. Butler, another friend, of it; but he did not seem to like it, as he wished me to stay at Ditton.

It so happened that shortly after this I was taken ill, and was obliged to be shut up in my room for two or three days, during which time I was ruminating in my own mind the conduct of the people at Ditton; how long I had preached among them, and how unwearied they had been in persecuting the gospel of Christ; and that, though God had cut off so many of them in their rebellion, yet they were still blind both to his mercies and to his judgments. As I had appeared in that place in the mean capacity of a coal-heaver, they would not allow themselves to think that God had sent such a one as me to preach to them. I then thought on my infirm state of body, and of the many weaknesses I labored under, which were brought on me by living abstemiously, and by hard labor, and that I was bringing my years "to an end like a tale that is told." And such is the policy of the devil that I believe he would counterfeit holiness, and tempt souls even to extreme abstinence, if he could by such means rid the world of an experienced believer, who he knows is a brazen wall and an iron tower against his interest; for such have weathered all his beseigers [sic] ever since the unjustifiable war was proclaimed by the devil against God. In short, I secretly wished that God would remove me from that place.

While musing in this manner it was suddenly impressed on my mind to leave Thames Ditton, and to take a house in London; that I should leave these little places in the country, and preach in the great metropolis, where hearers were more numerous; and that this was the meaning of the words that came to me in the vision, "Prophesy, son of man, prophesy on the thick boughs." Under this impulse I found myself very happy, and was thankful to God for my intended removal, it seemed to me so clearly to be of him. I then told the Lord that they hated me because of my poverty and mean appearance; when these words came to my mind with power, "A prophet is not without honor, save in his own country, and in his father's house." It was farther suggested to my mind that God had permitted them lately to persecute me more than usual, that they might wholly drive the gospel from them. And I much question if ever God sends his Word there again, for I think they are left almost as inexcusable as Chorazin and Capernaum, as no less than ten awful judgments had been conspicuously executed on them in their rebellion against the Word, as is related in my Naked Bow of God. And I believe, in less than two years after I left that place, there were no less than ten who were awfully destroyed by themselves or others. But to return. I then sent for a friend of mine, one Mr. Felton, and informed him of it; who said he thought me justifiable in leaving the place, observing also that a prophet has no honor in his own country. I then took my horse, rode to London, and informed some friends of it, every one of whom approved of my resolution. I accordingly took a house, and soon after ordered two carts from London to bring my household furniture from Ditton. Carts, I say, for I had no need of Joseph's wagons, as I had got but little in that inhospitable Canaan.

Five years of the term being unexpired of the lease of the house I was going to leave, I pondered in my own mind the impropriety of quitting before it was let, being fearful it would lie on my hands, and that I should want the money I had paid for the fixtures to carry with me, and what I had expended in planting the garden.

But my most blessed Banker provided against this trial also; for it came to pass, just as I had loaded my goods, that a person came and asked me if I had let my house. I told him "No." Upon which he replied, "I will take it of you, and buy your fixtures, your trees, and the garden crop also." In short, my landlord accepted him for his tenant, the lease was assigned over to him, the fixtures and plants appraised, the money paid down, the keys delivered up, and all was settled to my wish beyond all expectation. "Therefore, thou son of man, prepare the stuff for removings, and remove by day in their sight; and thou shalt remove from thy place to another place in their sight; it may be they will consider, though they be a rebellious house" (Ezek. xii. 3).

Thus far my vision appeared true. The next thing I had to observe was whether the boughs were *thick* or not; because the voice in the vision was, "Son of man, prophesy among the *thick* boughs." I then believed that the other part of the vision would be fulfilled, though all the world should oppose; and, having opened a larger chapel than I preached in at first, seemed still to confirm it more and more. I have now lived to see the boughs too thick for the chapel to contain them; and in this, as well as in everything else, I set to my seal "that God is true."

When I first began to open my mouth for the Lord, the master for whom I carried coals was rather displeased; at which I do not wonder, as he was a Pharisee of the Pharisees. I told him, however, that I should prophesy to thousands before I died; and soon after the doors began to be opened to receive my message. When this appeared, and I had left the slavish employment of coal-carrying, others objected to my master against such a fellow as me taking up the office of a minister. His answer was, "Let him alone, I once heard him say that he should prophesy to thousands before he died; let us see whether this prophesy comes to pass or not." He had, as I suppose, that passage in view mentioned by Moses, "And if thou say in thine heart, How shall I know the word which the Lord hath spoken? When a prophet speaks in the name of the Lord, if the thing follow not, nor come to pass, that is the thing which the Lord hath not spoken, but the prophet hath spoken it presumptuously; thou shalt not be afraid of him."

However, they very shortly saw that it came to pass, and in a very extraordinary manner too, for God opened four doors to me presently; and in a very little time brought me to preach out of the doors.

At my first beginning to speak in public, many professors and possessors of grace opposed me, as well as the world; some from a principle of jealousy; others from a principle of love, fearing that I should run before I was sent; but they knew not the impulse that I was under. Of their oppositions to me, however, I often complained to God in prayer, telling him that I expected some degree of support and encouragement from his own children; instead of which I had nothing but opposition, and a weakening of my hands. Indeed, some kept themselves at a distance from me, and have contradicted me at times, behaving quite insolent. In answer to my petitions the Lord applied these words to my heart, and gave me a strong faith in them: "A man's gift maketh room for him, and bringeth him before great men" (Prov. xviii. 16). At length I was led to see that I must be weaned from the church as well as from the world; and these words confirmed me in it, "Trust ye not in a friend; put ye no confidence in a guide; keep the doors of thy mouth from her that lieth in thy bosom" (Micah vii. 5). "The best of them is as a brier, the most upright is sharper than a thorn hedge" (Micah vii. 4).

God took an effectual method to convince many of his people of his having called me to the work of the ministry; for it so happened that a certain professor had engaged a minister to come from London and preach out of doors, at Moulsey on the Lord's day morning. This was published at our meetings, and as I had never heard a sermon out of doors, I was determined to go. As he was to preach at six o'clock in the morning, I could hear him without encroaching upon those hours in which our little church met. About three o'clock on the Lord's day morning I arose; but, as soon as I was out of bed, (pleasing myself at the thoughts of hearing a sermon, and having an opportunity of trying my doctrine by the standard of a London preacher), there came a voice to me with power, which I both heard and felt, saying, "You must preach out of doors to-day, and you must preach from this text, 'Go therefore into the highways, and as many as ye find, bid to the marriage'" (Matt. xii. 9). I was much amazed at this sudden impulse; yet I thought it was from God. If, however, I happened to mention any thing of the sort to some people, they would call it a delusion; but, notwithstanding this, God generally showed me afterwards that they themselves had but little, if any, experimental knowledge of God.

I shall now relate every circumstance of this extraordinary affair, and leave the unprejudiced to judge whether it was from God or from Satan. I sat down to look out the text, but could not find it. I then got up, and went to a friend about two miles off, who I knew had a little Concordance. I called him up, and asked him to look me out such a text, which he accordingly did. I turned it down, put my Bible into my pocket, and went with him to hear the gentleman that was to come from London. When we came to the place, I saw a great many people gathered together, and the table was set for the preacher to stand on; but behold he never came! So we waited till seven o'clock, when every one of those who had formerly opposed me, begged me to get up and preach. I could not but admire the divine conduct in this matter, that those who had opposed me (some because my language was bad; others, because they thought they had more understanding in the word than I had; others, because I was but a babe in grace, and they of long standing) were the very people who now invited me to preach. But here the cause of God was at stake, and there was now no answer in the mouth of any of those who had opposed me; therefore they forced that person up, whom they before had tried, by their conduct, to pull down. I complied with their request and went trembling up to my station. As soon, however, as my heart began to get warm in the cause, all my fears left me. I now delivered my message from the text God gave me, and he was with me in the work. Then it was that some were ready to cry, "Hosanna!" However, they had battered me about, that neither their applause nor their disapprobation had any weight with me. I often thought of the words spoken by Eliphaz to Job: "Call now, if there be any that will answer thee, and to which of the saints wilt thou turn?" (Job v. 1). Turn! turn to none but God, for, as the most upright among men is but as a brier, and sharper than a thorn hedge, we have no reason, like Abraham's ram, to hang our horns in a bush, lest we fall a sacrifice. "Cease from man, whose breath is in his nostrils," says the Almighty, "for wherein is he to be accounted of?" But there was a young widow who came to hear me preach that first sermon; and Providence opened her heart, so that she attended to the things spoken by the coal-heaver, and heard the gospel constantly afterward. At last she was seized with most violent convictions, being obliged to leave her place, and go home to Esher work-house, where a doctor was sent for to put a blister on her head; which is not a very proper remedy to draw out the bane of guilt, where the sting of death has so fatally envenomed the conscience. At times they found her quite delirious, and then she called earnestly on the Lord Jesus Christ. They then shook her, abused her for praying, and declared her mad; and when they found she had been among the Methodists, it was easily accounted for; therefore they handled her accordingly. But when she got a little better, she sent for me to come and pray by her, which I accordingly did; and then she told me of their cruel usage to her. I spoke to my wife about it; and we borrowed a bed, and got her home to our house. My wife nursed her body, and I tried to nurse her soul; soon after which she got well in body, and happy in mind. Then she took a lodging, worked for her bread, and continued to sit under my ministry for about six years. At last she fell into a deep decline, and soon took to her bed; and for two or three days before her death she was violently tempted and distressed, even beyond measure. After this she came forth from that dark cloud, shining like the rising sun; and continued in these blessed rays of glory till she closed her eyes in death, launching forth into eternity in all the triumph of a gospel conqueror. And here is the end of that mystery.

Chapter IX.

I WILL GIVE MY reader an account of another providence. A person came from Richmond to hear me preach at Ditton; and when he returned, informed several persons that he approved of my ministry. They accordingly sent me an invitation to come over to Richmond and help them; but I refused to go. However, they sent for me a second time, when I again refused. At last they went to the shoemaker I then worked for, who persuaded me to go, but not to preach in the chapel, but in a house that was licensed. I went very reluctantly indeed, but when I came there, I found the Lord's presence sweetly with me; and, at their request, I went again on the Tuesday following. Soon after I found I had done wrong in going there, though God had been powerfully with me; for it came to pass that tidings had been carried to London, and had reached the ears of two professing gentlemen, who were the managers of Richmond chapel. Whereupon they came down to Richmond to make inquisition whether any *coal-heaver* had ever presumed to preach the gospel to the poor souls at that place. Upon inquiry the thing was found to be certain, and the tidings were true; so the man and woman at whose house I had preached, received a very sharp reprimand, and were threatened also with the penal sum of fifty pounds, for letting me preach in their house, because I was not at that time properly licensed. Soon after this a day was appointed for preaching and prayer at Richmond chapel, and a dinner ordered at an inn for all the congregation that chose to dine there, and pay for it. Two ministers were appointed to preach on that occasion—after the commandments of men and not after Christ. An old gentleman took his text out of the Acts, and preached from these words: "And when Barnabas saw the grace of God he was glad," etc. Surely there was nothing in the text against my preaching at Richmond, for I was as glad to see the grace of God as ever Barnabas was. But he turned his text into a nose-of-wax, in order to make it fit my face; and told the people they might readily suppose that Barnabas had his credentials, or credential letters from the elders that were at Jerusalem; and so out of that supposition he spun a cat-o'-nine-tails to lash me with—a man whom he had never seen. But where I was to go for credentials I knew not; had he required credentials from God I could have produced them. Had I been there, I think I should have asked him whether that sermon had been from heaven or of men; however, at the long run, it appeared to be of men, because it came to naught. These things wonderfully distressed and puzzled me; first because the people sent three times after me before I would go at all; and, secondly, the presence and power of God seemed so visible to my comfort, and the comfort of those that heard me; and yet I was puzzled, that these great men, who were called Christians, should oppose me so much. The people, however, determined to hear me; and I generally found God with me in the work, notwithstanding which I always went reluctantly. In this matter I set off to an arm of flesh for counsel; though the presence of God was counsel sufficient, had I been wise enough to have rested on it. However, I was not as yet weaned from an arm of flesh; therefore I went to ask counsel at Abel, and so hoped to end the matter. The counsel I received from the good man I consulted (after I had related the whole circumstance to him) was, that I should stay away from preaching there, as it gave offense to some great men. I took his advice, and came home much eased in my mind, and glad that I could so get my neck out of the yoke. But, when the Tuesday following arrived, being the day on which I was appointed to preach at Richmond, I found the broken reed on which my foolish soul had rested began to give away, and I sunk again under all my distresses. Then it came into my mind how that God had comforted me in the work. And, if the supporting arm and comforting presence of God are not a sufficient testimony of God's approbation, we are not likely to get one from man. I still doubted, however, whether I should not offend God by trusting to this human counsel; thinking, if God had called me to preach at Richmond, and I should stay away when the little flock expected me, I should much offend the righteous Majesty of heaven, and be disobedient to the heavenly call; and, if it was wrong for me to go, I could appeal to God I had no desire for it. As to selfish views, I had none ; for one night they collected a parcel of money for me, knowing how poor I was, and how much I had suffered in the work; which they thrust into my pocket by force. But I positively refused it, and insisted on having no more than eighteen pence for my trouble in going from Ditton to Richmond to preach. It now came suddenly into my mind to lay this matter before my blessed Lord and Master, who never disappointed nor deceived me in his counsel. I therefore left my cobbling, went into my chamber, and prayed in the following manner: "Oh, God my Saviour and dear Redeemer, thou knowest I have no desire to go and preach at Richmond, but the people came after me several times. If thou hast any thing to do there by me, incline my heart to go, let who will oppose it; but, if not, let not thy servant presume, as my heart has no desire to go there; and, as I would not offend thy Majesty either by going or staying, I beseech thee to convince me by the first scripture that occurs to my mind. Oh, Lord, reveal thy mind and will to me in this particular, and let me not offend thee, as I am willing to obey thy voice, if thou art pleased to make it known to me. Amen."

As soon as I arose from my knees these words came with power to my mind, "Be not weary in well-doing, for in due time ye shall reap if ye faint not." This gave me some comfort. But, when I went and sat down to my cobbling again, I began to reason thus: "Be not weary in well-doing—true; but if it is displeasing to God for me to go to Richmond, then it would be well-doing to stay at home; and, if it be displeasing to God for me to stay at home, then it would be well-doing for me to go and preach at Richmond." So, like Gideon, I tried the fleece once more, and said to myself that, if God should give a text and a sermon on it, I should think it was from him, and that I had a just right to carry God's message. I had no sooner made this a criterion than these words came with power and understanding: "And his brightness was as the light; he had horns coming out of his hand, and there was the hiding of his power" (Hab. iii. 3, 4). The second and third verses of the thirty-third chapter of Deuteronomy I found were a key to this text. I therefore arose and went, being determined to deliver that message there at that time only, and then to inform them that I would come there no more. But before I began to preach I earnestly begged of God to comfort the people greatly, if he approved of my preaching to them; and, if not, that he would send them away dejected, and shut me up till I had little or nothing to say to them. In that night God blessed us wonderfully; and when I had done I hesitated whether I should inform them of my intention of not coming again, as it so offended the managers. But these words came to my mind: "And he said unto them, The kings of the Gentiles exercise lordship over them, and they that exercise authority upon them are called bene-factors. But ye shall not be so; but he that is greatest among you, let him be as the younger; and he that is chief as he that doth serve" (Luke xxii. 25, 26). Having received these words, I published myself to preach there again the next Tuesday, being fully convinced that no proprietor of a building had any warrant from God to keep a gospel message from the ears and hearts of God's children, unless they could prove the messenger either erroneous or wicked, which they could not, for they had never either seen or heard me.

After I had preached there a few times, it came to pass one evening, when I had finished my sermon, that a person came to inform me that a woman (who was lately taken very ill, and was apparently near death) desired to see me. I accordingly went; and, when I came to her bedside, asked her if she had sent for me. She replied, "Yes." I asked her for what she had sent for me to do. She said to pray for her. I asked her what I was to pray for—that she might be raised up again? She replied, "No, pray God to give resignation to his will, and that he may not depart from me." I asked her if she was sure the Lord was with her. She said, "Yes." I asked her how she came by the knowledge of God's comfortable presence. She told me she was a native of Scotland, where she had often heard people speak of their comforts and peace, but used to envy them for it, and at other times thought they spoke nonsense; but still she found a secret want of some-thing which she had long sought. She told me that she had never found that power until I preached the sermon from the text in Habakkuk, "He had horns coming out of his hands, and there was the hiding of his power." "Under that discourse," said she, "the Spirit of power came to me. My husband is a stone-mason, and is gone to Ireland to be the foreman of a very large building there, and I am in time to go after him, if God spares my life; but, as my good man has left me for a time, the Almighty has come in his room." She now gave me a very sweet account of the opera-tions of the Holy Ghost, and of the precious liberty which he proclaimed by the revelation and applica-tion of Christ crucified to her understanding mind and conscience. These tidings made my bowels yearn, as I could call to my remembrance the soul-travail I had been exercised with on the day that the text was brought to my mind, and the blessed mystery that was opened to me in it, as also God's goodness in accom-panying it with such power to her soul, and now to lay her on a sick bed, that she might send for me, to inform me that I had not preached nor travailed in vain. Oh, the conversion of such souls is greater riches to me than all the treasures of Egypt! God in mercy soon after raised her up again, and she attended my ministry for about two years, appearing a most ami-able Christian.

The conversion of this woman seemed to me such a testimony from God that it confirmed me more in my call to preach at Richmond than the testimony of all the divines in Britain would have done; for, "if we receive the witness of men, the witness of God is greater." I hope never to despise the former, but choose to stick close by the latter.

I shall now return to my subject of leaving Ditton and coming to settle in London.

After having seen so much of the vision fulfilled, I began to watch for the development of the words *thick boughs.* I knew thick boughs in Ezekiel's prophecy meant *sinners,* and the boughs of the palm-tree in the song of Solomon meant *saints;* therefore, if I could see my ministry well attended, either with sinners or saints, the whole vision would appear evidently to be from God; for, if the Lord speaks, it is done; and if he commands, it comes to pass.

After I had been some time in London, I found our chapel in Margaret street was open to every erroneous preacher. This stirred up the hearts of my hearers to look out for another place for me, and very soon a larger chapel was proposed to be built. This still appeared to pave the way more and more for the fulfillment of the words brought to my mind, "prophesy on the thick boughs." The chapel was soon erected, and the good hand of our God was with us in the work, to our comfort. But when it was opened I saw the strong opposition it would meet with from every quarter. This at first rather surprised me; but soon after these words returned on my mind, "prophesy on the thick boughs." I was enabled to rest on them, and gathered much comfort to my soul from the consideration of its being opposed; for I have ever observed that when a work has appeared to be of God, it has generally met with the greatest opposition; and when a cause flourishes in the face of many opposers, it appears still plainer to be God's work. The fewer human props there are to support the ark, the clearer God's hand is perceived; for then God appears to work, and none can let it though they try at it. In this way God, [*sic*] endears himself to the instrument he employs, weans the instrument from the creature, and secures all the glory to himself. I have often thought that if Martin Luther, John Bunyan, or George Whitefield had been alive in my days, they would rather have invited me than shut me out of their pulpits. However, I believe I shall still prophesy on the thick boughs; and according to my faith, so it will be unto me. I have found my very soul at times melted down with gratitude at the goodness of God to so unworthy a creature as myself, when I have heard that several good people in London have asked great men, employed under God, to let me preach in their pulpits, as Margaret street chapel was too small for me; but this favor could not be granted. I thought my case was similar to that of poor, sore-eyed Leah, who said, "The Lord saw that I was despised, therefore he gave me this son also." And I have now reason to conclude with her that God hath endowed me with a good dowry of spiritual children, though he saw that I was hated, and these spotted sheep shall be for my hire when they shall appear before the Lord; so shall the righteousness which I have preached answer for me in that day when my ministry and the seals of it shall appear before God to witness for me.

I will now inform my reader of the kind providence of my God at the time of building the chapel, which I named Providence chapel, and also mention a few free-will offerings which the people brought.

They first offered about eleven pounds, and laid it on the foundation at the beginning of the building. A good gentleman, with whom I had but little acquaintance, and of whom I bought a load of timber, sent it to me with a bull and receipt in full, as a present to the chapel of Providence. Another good man came with tears in his eyes, and blessed me, and desired to paint my pulpit, desk, etc., as a present to the chapel. Another person gave half a dozen chairs for the vestry, and my friends, Mr. and Mrs. Lion, furnished me with a tea-chest well stored, and a set of china. My good friends, Mr. and Mrs. Smith, furnished me with a very handsome bed, bedstead, and all its furniture and necessaries, that I might not be under the necessity of walking home in the cold winter nights. A daughter of mine in the faith gave me a looking-glass for my chapel study. Another friend gave me my pulpit cushion, and a book-case for my study. Another gave me a book-case for the vestry. And my good friend, Mr. E., seemed to level all his displeasure at the devil; for he was in hopes I should be enabled, through the gracious arm of the Lord, to cut Rahab in pieces; therefore he furnished me with a sword of the spirit, a new Bible, with morocco binding and silver clasps.

But I shall show that I have yet to speak on the behalf of Providence, which was so conspicuous in furnishing me with money necessary for building the chapel. I never went to one person to borrow money for the building who denied me. God so opened their hearts that I was amazed at his providence and their kindness towards me.

Some time after these things, God seemed wholly to withdraw his conspicuous providential acts; and I began to lay aside my watchfulness and daily dependence on his bounties, as my stated income began to be tolerable. However, it is the safest and sweetest way to live from hand to mouth, as say those who speak in proverbs; for it is impossible that men should be so grateful to God when they have a stock in hand as when they receive a daily supply from the never-failing stock in God's hand. After some little time I was forced to look to him again for temporals as well as spirituals; for as my income increased, my family increased also; so that I was shortly brought into as great straits as ever; money began to run short, and clothes were wanting. But God, who fainteth not, neither is weary, was pleased to appear in a way of providence again, and after this manner showed he himself.

I had been doing a little work in my flower garden, and finding that it wanted a few additional roots, I went to a garden at a little distance from my house to look over a few things. While I was walking about by myself among the flowers, a well-dressed motherly-looking woman stepped up to me, and supposing me to be the gardener (for my appearance was more like a slave than a prelate), she thus addressed me in a free and jocose manner, "Now, Mr. Gardener, if you please, I want a root to put in my pot; and it must be a root that will last." I looked up very seriously at the lady, and replied. "Well, I believe I can tell you where you may get such a root." At this answer she smilingly asked, "Where?" I answered, "In the book of Job; for he says, 'The root of the matter is found in me' (Job xix. 28). And if you can get that root into your pot, both the root and the pot will last for ever." She then asked, "And pray have you got that root in you?" I answered her, "I verily believe I have." Upon which she replied, "It is well with you, and it is very true what you have said." I then told her that I was not the gardener, but that she would find him at the bottom of the garden, attending some ladies and gentlemen. She dropped a courtesy, and departed with a smile. I thought, by her pertinent reply, that she was not altogether ignorant of that "wisdom which dwells with prudence, and finds out knowledge of witty inventions" (Prov. viii. 12). And I secretly wished that the words which I had spoken might dwell on her mind until the root of gospel love struck an everlasting fiber in her heart.

I believe the lady above mentioned inquired of the gardener who I was; for soon after both she and her spouse came to hear me, and have continued so to do ever since. God grant that the word of his grace may take deep root in their hearts, that they may be "trees of righteousness, the right-hand planting of God, that he may be glorified."

Some time after this there came a person to my house, and left a letter, the contents of which were as follows:

"SIR, —

"I wish you would be at home on such a day, if convenient; as a person will call to measure you for a great coat; which you are desired to accept, and to ask no questions of the person who comes to measure you," etc.

I looked upon this letter sent from some enemy to the gospel of Christ; because it came soon after my Bank of Faith had made its appearance in the world; and I daily heard of some professor or other ridiculing it, because I had therein taken notice of very insignificant things, at least in their opinion. However, had they been exercised with a hungry belly, as the prophet Elijah was, they would have been glad of a cake baked with two sticks, and have thanked God for commanding the widow woman to sustain him with that (I Kings xvii. 9). The Holy Ghost through this kind providence of God, which appeared in sending the prophet that cake, thought this worthy of divine revelation; if so, of what kind of spirit must those professors be who deem the special and minute interference of Providence worthy only of their public scorn and contempt? Such men are rebuked even by the brute creation; for "the ox knoweth his owner, and the ass his master's crib," but the carnal professor knoweth not the God of his mercies; and although he loves the crib, yet he doth not consider who it is that keeps his crib full.

I was deceived in supposing that the letter was sent as a trap to keep me at home on such a day, that they might have to laugh at my vain expectation, as I conjectured; for it was sent by a friend; and the man came as was appointed to measure me for a great coat. I asked who sent him. He told me that was to be kept secret. But, as I suspected the letter to be a cheat sent by some enemy, I insisted on knowing who sent him. He then said that he was sent by a woman who once asked me for a root to put in her pot. I told him that I had got two very good great coats, but stood in need of a close-bodied one; and, if the lady thought proper to make me a present of such,

I should be obliged to her; but that I had no need of a great coat. The man measured me, and brought me the coat home. I offered him a small present for his trouble, but he refused it saying that he had received orders not to take any thing. Christian reader, give God the glory for his wonderful works, and let not *fortune* and *luck* rob him of his honor. "Jesus we know, but who are they?"

When I laid the foundation of the chapel I was twenty pounds in debt for the necessaries of life, and when I had finished it I was in arrears one thousand pounds more; so that I had plenty of work for faith, if I could but get plenty of faith to work ; and while some deny a Providence, Providence was the only resource I had. I had forty-seven pounds per annum ground rent, and almost fifty pounds per annum for the interest, a large chapel, and a small congregation; and those who lent me the money a poor, industrious people, and weak in faith, being but young in the ways of God. There were plenty of hypocrites in Zion to tell them that all who had a hand in that chapel would burn their fingers. If God sends Moses and Aaron to preach, Satan sends Jannes and Jambres to oppose; and if Zerubbabel and Joshua begin to build, Sanballat and Tobiah are raised up to discourage them. And here I must bring in a circumstance which is truly laughable. A gentleman had for some time frequented Margaret-Street Chapel, and to all appearance was a very penitent hearer, as he was generally bedewed with tears; but whether they were tears of misery from a sense of sin, or tears of gratitude from a sense of pardon, I knew not; but I have been convinced since that they were neither. This good gentleman came to us when the chapel was in building, and hearing the builder say he should want some window sills, and some columns to stand in the cellar to support the ground floor, he generously offered his service to go into the country to buy them, as he had formerly been in the wood way himself. This kind offer was gratefully accepted; and another gentleman offered him his horse to go on. He accordingly received his orders of the length of the columns, the size of the heart at the small end, and that they must be the ground ends of young trees, able to support the weight they were intended to bear. So off he went, and in a day or two returned, and informed several of my friends that he had saved me three pounds by the journey, which to me was something considerable. Soon after his return the timbers came, but by no means fit for the purpose they were designed, being only the limbs of large oaks, small, and not one straight among them. The builder appeared disgusted at them, and ordered the carter to reload them and take them home to his own house, which he accordingly did. The builder then went over the water and bought a fine, large, straight stick, at the price of nine pounds, and intended to cut it into proper lengths and quarter it; which when, our kind friend saw, he got a cart and brought his materials back again, and threw them down on the premises, which rather hindered than helped us. He then delivered the bill to me, which, to the best of my remembrance, was five pounds seven shillings, which, with three pounds that he had saved me by the bargain, made them worth eight pounds seven shillings. I offered to pay his bill, and to make him a present of the timber if he would accept it; but he would not, nor could we use it; so that this good man's favors became a hinderance rather than a help. At last I resolved to have them valued, and sent for a timber merchant, who attended me to value them. He valued them at two guineas. But thinking the gentleman might undervalue them through partiality to me, I sent for an entire stranger, who was a timber merchant also, and he fixed their price at forty shillings. Upon this my good friend took the materials away, and for this price he sold them, clearly much less for himself than he saved me. But to return to my subject. These were the difficulties I had to surmount; and for three years together I lost ground, for Satan waylaid me in a path which I knew to be charity. My bowels were moved to extricate from debt a man that I took to be a fallen saint, nor could all the inward checks God gave me stop me from embarking in this good work, though I had many. He cost me forty guineas; and when God unmasked the hypocrite, then I saw where the inward caution came from. Three chapels were opened about the same time not far from mine, and one set up an additional lecture, in order to keep the sheep from straying; but the inward anointing taught me that by these means I should see more clearly the hand of God, for where there is no opposition there is no salvation; and where multitude of hands are employed in one work, it is not so easy to see the distinguishing approbation of the employer. I must stand alone, and work alone, that I might not say a confederacy, nor rely on human aid. Paul's companions all forsook him at Nero's bar, that by him the preaching might be fully known; for Paul's doctrine was immediately from Christ, but theirs immediately from him.

After this blank of forty guineas loss, another borrowed three more, and another ten pounds, neither of which ever paid a mite again; and soon after thirty pounds were demanded for the follies of my youth, and another thirty pounds for rent for the chapel I had left; and thirty guineas more for a lawsuit about a little meeting house for which I had collected forty pounds to build at Sunbury, in Middlesex. All these blanks, at three years' end, set me down just where I began; and all this time my income was only twenty-five pounds per quarter, and my children at one time nine in number. This sailing against wind and tide not only tried the faith of the debtor, but it exercised the faith of my poor creditors also, for if I could not go on, they must go back. Nevertheless, most of them exercised more patience than I could, though I could do no more than just keep the interest paid up.

At length God enabled me to put out several little books, which were almost universally exclaimed against, both by preachers and professors, and by these means God sent them into all winds; so that I soon rubbed off one hundred, and soon after another, so that in a short time I had reduced my thousand pounds down to seven hundred. The booksellers in general would neither countenance nor circulate the works, being influenced, as I suppose, by some of their employers. But as the workman began to be known, so the works spread; and what some despised others admired; and the doctrine that starved the self-sufficient fattened the poor in spirit. People who attended my ministry, coming from various parts of the country, often bought them, and sent them down among their friends. By these means they made their way where I was not permitted to go myself. But it often happened that where they came the preachers warned the people much against them, which frequently excited the curiosity of some to read them; and if they found any thing in them that suited their cases, they judged by the unction they felt. They are calculated in some measure to suit the earnest inquirer; the soul in bondage, in the furnace, in the path of tribulation, or in the strong hold of Satan; and I have heard of them from Wales, from Scotland, from Ireland, from various parts of America, from Cadiz in Spain, from Alexandria in Egypt, and I believe from both the East and West Indies. And as they have fallen in divers hands, I accordingly received various reports; many vilifying and scurrilous letters from different parts, and, to counterbalance these, many letters of blessings to God and thanks to the author; which, put together, make it to be the good old beaten path: "through evil report and good report, as deceivers and yet true."

Chapter X.

As THE CHAPEL FILLED, and the people approved, of course my pedigree, my residence, my station in the camp, my family and fortune, were inquired into; and that at a time when some of my creditors wanted their money. In a short time after this demand, a small number of gentlemen offered to lend me one hundred pounds, without either note of hand or interest; and, being a little from each of them, they took it as God prospered me, till all was cleared. But poor men's difficulties, like woman's work, are never done, for soon after fifty pounds more was called in, besides many little debts which were contracted while the former sums were paying off; so that I was encompassed about with a whole crowd of creditors, and who can expect less who make themselves debtors to all? A gentleman of the city, who had a little house at Peckham, asked me to go on a week-day evening to preach in that neighborhood, and to take a supper and bed at his house, which I agreed to; and, being without either purse or scrip, gold or silver, when I set off, I called on my invaluable and never-failing friend, Mr. Baker, of Oxford street, and asked him if there was any of the chapel money in his hands. To my great comfort he told me, No; so I borrowed a few shillings and set off. But, that I might give vent to my grief, and bemoan my hard fate in secret, I called a coach, and got in, the devil following me. So we went together, and I had not one six-penny or shilling debt in all the world but what the devil set before me, together with various prisons for poor debtors; and aggravated my misery by setting before me the power of God to help me if he would, the wealth that he gave to many wicked persons, and his hard dealings with those that loved him. But at length recollecting myself, I bantered the devil. I said, "Satan, hast thou got any cash by thee? if thou hast, bring it. I do not care where you get it, bring it if you have any, I will receive it, and thank God for it; but, if thou art as poor as myself, let my debts alone." The devil left me at this. *"Resist the devil,"* says God, *"and he will flee from you;"* and so he did, and my soul was delivered as a roe from the hand of the hunter, or as a bird from the hand of the fowler. When I came to the end of St. George's Fields, I got out and walked the rest of the way, and that night had a glorious time in the Lord's work. Satan had for a season left me and I returned in the power of the Spirit. I spent a comfortable evening with my friends, and had a most uncommon time in prayer by myself at going to bed, and a most sweet frame of meekness, gratitude, and godly sorrow, given me when in bed; in the morning I arose sweetly becalmed, and much resigned to the will of God. However, on my way home, the old serpent set at me again; but, having found faith strong in exercise over night, he could not make those inroads on my soul as he had done the day before. I called on my dear friends, Mr. and Mrs. Baker, and told them that I should shortly have a liftup, as I usually called it; and that I had got it already in faith, and should shortly have it in hand. On the next Sunday morning a gentleman of the city came into the vestry to me, with a bank note in his hand, and gave it to me, saying, "I am desired to give you that." I asked who it came from. He replied, "You do not know the person; you never spoke to him but once; but he told me that it was strong upon his mind that you was in want, and he put it into his pocket for you last Thursday, and it had burnt in it ever since, but he knew not how to convey it to you." That same Thursday was the day Satan had beset me so violently; and while Satan was reproaching me with my debts, God's good Spirit was preaching to that gentleman to lessen them. Upon this a gentleman to whom God had made me useful, generously offered to lend me eighty pounds to answer my present demands, and to take it of me as I could pay it; this I gladly accepted, and then answered the present demand of those gentlemen who at times stood in need of their money. At this time a gentleman from Bristol came frequently to hear me, and invited me to that place; to which I consented, and was to have a letter previous to the time of my going thither. After some time waiting, the letter came, and when it came my pocket was empty; but at that juncture a letter came from a lady in the country, with a twenty-pound note in it. With part of this I took my journey to Bristol, as Joseph and Mary took theirs to Egypt with the wise men's gold presented to Christ in the stable. Soon after my return, I, one night, in my discourse in the city, opened my mind freely and scripturally upon the use and end of the law of God, describing who were under it and who not. A great man, next to a great woman, happened to be there, who had light enough to see my darkness, and from that time sounded the alarm, and preached up the law, till he was ten times blinder than I was. This alarm spread, and most pulpits rang with warnings against antinomianism. This terrified the people, and many fled from me; some halted, and some few abode. However, the continual warnings on every hand soon reduced a crowded audience to a very small number, and the longer I preached the fewer I had, till I was sure the small number could not defray the expenses attending the lecture. And now was the time for my old enemy to work. He condemned my doctrine; which I did not wonder at, as an accuser has nothing to work upon but sin, nor anything to work by but a broken law, for where there is no law there is no transgression, and where there is no transgression there can be no accusation. He harassed me with the great number of divines all against me, with my debts also, with the invisible disapprobation of God by the almost general absence of the whole congregation; and, last of all, that my own poor pocket must defray the expenses of the place, and that money was the property of others, and it is the wicked that borrow and pay not again. That Tuesday was a day of darkness and gloominess to me. However, I replied, that God was not tied to that congregation, he could discharge the debts I should contract by keeping open that place many other ways, and therefore I determined to continue there till there were but ten to hear. That night the number was much greater than the time before; and the same night I received a letter with these words, "Sir, I have the honor of being a steward to your Master, and am at times intrusted with a trifle for the benefit of his servants, and I know of none more worthy than yourself." And that was all, except a ten-pound note, which bore me through that quarter; and from that night we increased, till the house was filled with guests. "Bless the Lord, O my soul, and all that is within me bless his holy name."

Being informed that the house I then dwelt in was to be sold, and being desired by my landlord to admit any person into it that came, unsettled my mind exceedingly, interrupted me in my studies and in my writing. However, sold it must be, and sold it was; and I, being a tenant at will, must prepare my stuff for removing. Some of my friends attended the sale on my behalf, but the price ran too high. As it was but a leasehold, a person in the neighborhood, a possessor of much money and a professor of religion (who was resolved to have it), bought it for himself and family. I had expended a few pounds in paving the walk to the door and the yard behind the house, which the auctioneer said should be paid to me, but that pay never came.

Some few days were spent in looking after a house, and at length one presented itself which was empty, and had stood empty for some time; the rent was double to that which I was leaving, that being twenty pounds per annum, this forty. Nevertheless I took it, longing to be settled somewhere. I got the keys, and immediately began to move, though it was six or seven weeks before the time expired of my other house, for the which I must pay rent, having entered upon that quarter. When I had removed all my goods I lent the gentleman who had bought the premises the keys of the house, that he might get it in order for his own reception, for which he was much pleased and kindly thanked me; but he soon requited me for my kindness by sending me an attorney's letter for taking up a little favorite tree which I had planted. Satan, upon this, tempted me to take out my knife and cut off another of my own planting close by the ground. But vengeance belongeth to God, and he will repay; and so I found it, for in less than nine months my successor and his wife were both in their graves, and the house sold again. They removed me, and God removed them.

My new habitation being so much larger than the other,

my little furniture was almost lost in it. However, the unerring and never-failing providence of God, which has, in uniformity with his word promise, incessantly followed me and presided over me all my days, most conspicuously appeared at this time also. A lady in the country sent me, in a letter, a forty-pound bank note. A gentleman in the city gave me a handsome new bureau and two mahogany elbow chairs. Another gentleman sent me a new handsome chamber chair with stuffed back and sides, and a handsome cover and cushion. While another, who came to see my new habitation, said, "My friend, I think you want a carpet for this large room," and left me a ten-pound note to purchase one. And here I must set up mine Ebenezer, and say, with a pious prophet of old, "Hitherto hast the Lord helped us."

But this stream of prosperity must not continue. I must be tried, I must learn my doctrine in the furnace of affliction, and fetch my sermons from God's powerful application and my own soul's experience, that I may be at a point and speak with authority, and that my hearers may see God's fatherly goodness and severity follow me and work in me, as well as hear an account of it from me. I fell sick, and lay for some time; and for three or four years, one after another. I had much sickness in my family, and my doctor's bills of course came heavy. Besides one young child at wet-nurse, I had five more at school, and three, one after another, lately dead. I had my eldest daughter at a school at Greenwich, and her governess gained the applause of many persons for her liberality to me, who averred that she educated my child for nothing, though I paid her sixteen guineas per annum for her all the time she was there, with one guinea earnest at her going, which was two guineas per annum more than she had for one-half of her scholars. A little boy, which I had at wet-nurse at Walworth, was much desired by a gentlewoman in that neighborhood, as soon as it was proper to wean him; which desire I granted, and she dry-nursed him, and had him for three or four years. She also gained the esteem of many of my friends for keeping one of my children gratis, because of my large family; but God knows that I paid her after the rate of twenty pounds per annum for every day she kept him. Thus some made the miraculous providence of God to favor me where it never appeared, while others denied the whole of it, and some burnt the relation of it where it really did.

About this time I called upon my dear and unwearied friends, Mr. and Mrs. Baker, of Oxford street, who, from the time God first made me manifest in their consciences to the present moment, never failed me, forsook me, nor turned their backs on me. For while the chapel was building, when money was continually demanded, if there was one shilling in the house I was sure to have it. God never suffered their souls to get one morsel of the bread of life but under me; and it is seldom that one quarter has rolled over my head, for these sixteen years, but what I have stood in need of some assistance from them; thus God tied us together.

At the same time God sorely tried them by various losses in business, by bankruptcies and bad debts continually; and, to add a little more fire to the furnace, a very near relation in the flesh fell into insanity, who has been confined in a private mad-house at their expense for many years, and is still on their hands, as I and my concerns were many years on their backs; but still God supported them, comforted them, and kept their souls alive in their trouble.

A large sum of money was now demanded of one of my creditors, and it was demanded in haste, being wanted. At this time my pocket had been well drained for furniture, and many more things were still wanting; however, the sum must be had, and it was one hundred and sixty pounds. My heart sunk at the sound. "James," says I, "what shall I do?" "Do," says he, "you shall pay it. The woman that has called it in does not want it, she receives her interest, and is in no danger of losing the principal; the devil has stirred her up on purpose to plague you." But I replied, "James, where shall I get one hundred pounds?" "Why," said he, "you shall have it of James Baker." "Why," said I, "have you one hundred to spare?" "Yes," said he, "one hundred more; it lies by itself. It cost me eighty pounds in, and it is a good time to sell out." And he sold it out for one hundred and one pounds. The rest we made up, and I carried it to the person who demanded it, and she purchased two hundred pounds stock, which cost her two hundred and two pounds. Thus my dear friend cleared twenty-one pounds by serving me, and she lost as much by distressing me.

God took away another of my poor children; it died at my friend Chapman's, at Petersham, and was buried in the same ground where we since have erected our tomb. Upon the back of the disaster I fell sick, and lay some time. Soon after my little daughter was brought home from school with a violent fever, which continued on her many months; but after my faith and patience had been a little tried, God raised her up again. Some time after a fever broke out in the school where my sons were, and three of them came home, one of whom was ill, and had a fit of sickness; so that in a short time I had sixty or seventy pounds to pay to different gentlemen of the faculty, for attendance on me and them. Add to this another fifty pounds of borrowed money was called in; not for want of it, but for private pique. This we made shift to get together and informed the person where to call for it; but it lay a long time before it was called for. The grief was not from fear of losing it, but at my being able to procure it. But my God now appeared again: a friend in the city gave me thirty pounds, another soon after sent me twenty pounds, and two more gave me forty pounds;

and an elderly gentleman, who had for some time attended my ministry, and who had been a member of a church in the city for many years—but I have reason to believe that it pleased God to revive the work in his soul under me, for he at times called on me and acknowledged as much, and often lamented that this world had for a long time obscured the good work on him,— soon after this he left this world, leaving me fifty pounds by will, and several more legacies, as I have been informed, to other indigent persons.

I could now compare creditor and debtor together, and see a balance in my own favor; so that I had no fears about me that any one friend would lose any thing by me, should it please God to remove me. I had also given forty pounds premium at the binding of one of my sons, and twenty pounds more to a mantua-maker with my elder daughter. I had for some years been Jack at everybody's call, being invited to preach collection sermons continually, and wherever I went this was sure to be the case; sometimes I was to collect for the minister, sometimes to rub off the debt of the buildings; sometimes for the poor; but always for something or for somebody, and I was generally desired to give it out at my own chapels, as their hopes were more in the pockets of my followers than in their own. A meeting which had not long been erected within a few miles of Uxbridge, in Middlesex, had a debt upon it which the people wished to clear off, and therefore proposed to have two sermons preached on a certain day annually, and a collection at each sermon, as the best method of extricating the chapel out of debt; and of course I was once invited thither upon this business. I travelled at my own expense, and was entertained by a friend of my own at Uxbridge. I preached in the forenoon, and a gentleman from London was to preach in the afternoon, and if I was rightly informed, my collection was fourteen pounds; what the gentleman got I know not, as I went off as soon as I had finished my discourse. The year following a minister of yearly fame was invited, who promised either to go himself or to send his curate, upon these conditions, namely, that they would promise him "never to suffer that fellow Huntington to preach among them any more;" which request the principal person of the meeting submissively listened to, and promised to admit me there no more. "Who can stand before envy?" Upon these conditions the good man promised either to go or to send; but at the same time observed that the traveling expenses must be borne, which was making a sure bargain, and in which the vicar displayed more wisdom that I did; and this they agreed to also, knowing, as every man must, that the laborer is worthy of his hire. The time came round for another anniversary, and the curate went and preached and enforced the collection; and when the preacher's entertainment, traveling expenses, etc., were defrayed, there remained *two pence* towards the debt of the chapel. Neither their promise nor the conscience would ever suffer them again to invite me, and as for the curate, they found him (in money matters) to be an unprofitable servant, and therefore they took counsel, and laid the anniversary aside from that day forward; which was a better work in the sight of God than that of bringing it into use.

I was formerly often invited to preach at a meeting in Little St. Helens, where I preached at seven o'clock on the Lord's Day morning. That lecture had been long established for the benefit of servants, who by reason of their domestic employ, could not attend the service of God at the usual times of public worship. The person who invited me informed me that most of the supporters of that lecture were dead, and that whenever they had a collection sermon for it they seldom got more than twenty or thirty shillings. Hearing these things, I therefore promised to go, and was well attended. Not long after, I was

invited again, and the place was so crowded that great
numbers could not get in; and, as I was informed, I collected ten pounds. I inquired at last, as they came frequently to ask me to preach, who the ministers were that
preached the lectures, and they told me their names, but
I knew none of them; and farther, that they had a guinea
a time for preaching, and that they were board-ministers
or ministers belonging to the board. But I was not a
board-minister; therefore the lecture had my labor gratis;
my office was to preach the guineas together, while that
of the board-ministers was to preach them away. I
thought of a story that I once heard, namely, of a man
putting potatoes into the fire to roast, while a monkey
sitting before it observed him. The monkey wanted the
potatoes, but fearing to burn his own paw, took the fore-
foot of the cat to rake it out of the fire, whilst he ate it
himself. Whoever was the monkey, I was the cat. At length
I got sick of this. Nevertheless they came again, and entreated me to come and give them another sermon. I replied. "There is to be a collection, I suppose." They answered, "Oh, yes, sir." I replied, "I have no doubt of it;
but depend upon it I will be your cat's paw no longer,"
and I saw them no more. But soon after I heard the lecture was dropped, though I think it might have been kept
up to this day, if the board-men had labored on as rea-
sonable terms as I did. Some years I toiled up and down
in this way, preaching collections for one minister or another. "Everywhere, and in all things, I am instructed,"
says Paul. And so am I, for the vicar's bargain for his
curate, and the board-men leaving off when money failed,
brought me a determination not to labor for nothing, —
especially, having been sitting at home while I have been
preaching for them, who have ridiculed me after I had
begged money; and well they might, for who but a fool,
when God has used a shepherd to collect a flock together,
would lead that flock from post to pillar, on purpose to

shear them, and give the wool to men whom I know not whence they be? Bless my God, these board-men have taught me better things. I keep my flock at home, and shear them for my own profit; and sure none can have so much right to the wool as those who labor day and night to feed the sheep, and I have vanity enough to think that they had rather the profits of the fleece fell to my share than to any other. Many journeys of one hundred, two hundred, or three hundred miles, which have cost ten, twenty, or thirty pounds a journey, have I travelled, and at the same time paid one pound five shillings per week for a supply at home in my absence; but I confine my labors now, not to every place where I am invited, but where I am well known, and where there are poor hungry souls to feed; to these my mouth is open, and to me their heart is. God has not sons of peace in every house.

Chapter XI.

MY CONGREGATION BEGAN GREATLY to increase, and the heat of the place in times of service began to be almost unbearable; it was of course thought necessary to enlarge the chapel. Now there was a spare bit of ground, which lay about the middle of the chapel against the east wall, the dimensions of which were thirty feet by twenty-five, and this spare morsel of ground had nothing on it but a shed; this ground we endeavored to get, and intended to break through on that side the chapel, and so to throw the chapel into a triangular form, and to move the pulpit to the centre of the gallery on the west side, that it might face the new-intended erection. The gentleman who held this ground by lease was applied to; and he, in company with a builder, met with me and a few friends of mine, and intimated that he was willing to accommodate us. Of course we wished to know his terms, or what he expected for ground-rent, and he told us his price was one hundred guineas per annum. And so I found it, and they are determined to make the most of it. I have been informed, but I cannot avouch it, that all the ground on which that oblong pile of buildings stands within the compass of the four streets, of which my chapel is a part, pays no more to his Grace, the Duke of Portland, than fourteen pounds a year; but, if it was all to be let in the same proportion as was demanded of me, it could not, I think, bring in less than ten thousand pounds per annum. But, as Canaan was to be a servant of servants, so I must have been a tenant of tenants. Finding nothing could be done with the *earth-holders,* I turned my eyes another way, and determined to build my *stories in the heaven* (Amos ix. 6), where I should find more room and less rent; and to this my friends agreed. [*sic*] namely, to raise the chapel one story higher, and to carry a flight of galleries all round it. The next thing was to find a man to execute this design, and one was soon found capable of the undertaking. But what I wanted to get at most, was whereabouts the expense would be. Besides, my shoulders having been kept raw for seven or eight years together, and it was but lately that they had begun to heal, and remaining exceedingly sore and tender, I was more afraid of another burden than I was of the heat of the day, lest it should terminate in an abscess, and I should be left to the accusations of the devil as an incurable. But, when the expense was named, it did not appear so alarming. He told me he thought it would amount to four hundred pounds; this was a shoeing-horn, only to draw me on. But, as the person often sat under me as a hearer, I thought it was not likely that one who could face the rays of light, and stand the force of truth, would, or could, willingly and wilfully deceive a servant of Christ; "But their inward thought and heart is deep" (Ps. lxiv. 6); "sharper than a thorn hedge" (Micah vii. 4).

> "When wisdom wakes
> Suspicion sleeps at wisdom's gate,
> And up to simplicity resigns her charge:
> Where Goodness thinks no ill where no ill seems."
> (MILTON.)

We must not measure everybody's corn by our own bushel; those who can make the ephah small and shekel great will abide by their own standard, till they have filled up the measure of the fathers.

However, we began and went on with the work. Hitherto, I had not only the care of the church, the care of a large family, and for a long time the principal care of the poor, till they made me poorer than themselves, but I had, also, the whole burden of chapel debt, and ten thousand cares how to get that burden off. Many, perceiving that it was with the greatest reluctance that I bowed my shoulders the second time, advised me to try the liberality of my friends, and to see if they would not put their shoulders to the work. To this I readily agreed; but we determined to move only in the circle of our own acquaintance, or to call upon such, and only such, as attended my ministry, leaving other ministers to enjoy their own fleece; and by this rule we abode; into any other little hill of Zion, into the way of the Gentiles, or into any of the cities of the Samaritans, we entered not. To begging, therefore, we went; and as the work of the chapel went on, so I saw more and more the necessity of pursuing this calling, for I shortly perceived that I was in the hands of a man who could have no feeling for my shoulders, nor any more mercy upon my pocket than an angry God will have upon a hypocrite in Zion; and, to the honor of God and the credit of his people be it spoken, there was not one we visited that frowned upon us, or that showed an angry countenance, or that sent us empty away. They were as generous to me with their pocket as I am to them with a springing cruse in the pulpit. and we found begging to be a delightful employ. Besides, God kept us so happy in visiting the brethren that we sowed many spiritual things while we reaped carnal, so that they were as glad to see us as we were to rob them; and after a few of these trading tours we came to a conclusion of the business; and when we sat down under the hedge, and had put the money into our hats, and had counted it up, we found it to amount to the total sum of seven hundred pounds; "so mightily grew the word of God and prevailed," not only over books of curious arts, but over the root of all evil. But all this wonderful and unexpected liberality was far from being sufficient to enable me to go upright; "I must still bow my shoulders to bear, and become a servant of tribute" (Gen. xlix. 15). For, when the work was finished, and the bills brought in, the four hundred was swelled to that degree that it amounted to one thousand two hundred and thirty pounds! I believe it to be the best job, and the worst, that ever he took in hand. I cannot forget it, nor do I believe that ever he will. By these exorbitant charges my debts were greatly increased; but the reason he assigned for it was, that I had given the men so much victuals and drink that they wasted much of his time in consuming it; and, though he and his sons shared in my liberality, yet he made me redeem the time they lost, because my bounty was evil; nevertheless, I would sooner bear the burden of a thousand such bills than the weight of such a builder's conscience. The remains of my old debt were upwards of three hundred pounds; this new addition was five hundred and thirty, and these, together with small debts contracted while this work was doing (besides my liberality to the men), made the weight of my future burden amount to about nine hundred pounds. With this load I began my second stage; but before I had travelled far an additional weight was added. I had got together one hundred pounds, and I had it in my pocket, intending in a day or two to pay it away. A friend of mine (falsely so called) knew this, and on the Lord's day morning came into the vestry to me, and informed me that a person whom I respected was going to be arrested for the small sum of sixty pounds, and pressed me hard to lend him the money I then had in my pocket. I told him I was altogether a stranger to the gentleman's circumstances. "But," says he, "I am not, and had I a thousand pounds I would lend it him." I replied, "I have no objection to lend it to you." Upon this a friend in the vestry interfered, and took him to task for dragging the money from me. Nevertheless, he followed me up; but I still replied, "I am willing to lend it to you." And at last he replied, "Well, do then." So I gave it to him. In the evening he came into the vestry to me, with such a countenance as I shall never forget, and put a scrap of paper doubled up down upon the table, and departed; which, when I examined, I found to be the gentleman's note, not his own. In a few days after, the gentleman failed in business and went to prison, and then the whole matter came to light. The person who was in danger of losing the sixty pounds was brother-in-law to him who squeezed the money from me; so that the plan was well laid, and well executed. He that pressed me to lend the money was worth some thousands himself, and so was he that got in his sixty pound debt, and I had one hundred pounds more added to the other nine, which set me down within twenty or thirty pounds of the same sum with which I started at first. "The men of this world are in their generation wiser than the children of light;" and yet one child of light is wiser than all the men of this generation.

Finding this recruiting of the burden to sit very heavy, except at times when much favored with the presence of God, and it being such a matter for the old accuser to work upon in every time of trouble, I determined to take an account of my books, I mean my own publications; and when this was done, and the value of the stock cast up, I found I had eight hundred pounds worth of books, and the stationer and printer both clear. I resolved with myself to part with them, and with my copyright; and here I had various struggles between feeling for self and feeling for others. I thought, on the one hand, that my books might be of some service to the large family I might leave behind, never expecting to leave them anything else; and, on the other hand, being continually in debt was a sore burden, and the fears of dying so would not suffer me at times to sleep. I therefore resolved to part with them; but then who to apply to was the next thing to be considered; and I knew that whoever bought them had need of some money, as some of them would lie along on their hands, which I also considered; and afterwards I fixed the price in my own mind, which was four hundred pounds, no more nor less; and then I mentioned it to a gentleman of the city, who agreed to take them, and who paid me the money; and this reduced my debt to somewhat less that six hundred pounds.

Soon after this, the gentleman who failed in business above mentioned, who had my hundred pounds, sent me fifty pounds of it back again, which was all he could ever pay, and this was more than I ever expected. A kind friend of mine, at the other end of the town, about this time gave me twenty pounds, and another sent me ten pounds; and now I was enabled to diminish my debt to the sum of five hundred pounds; and there it remained for a long time, without either addition or diminution. In the meantime I continually entreated the Lord to let his goodness pass before me, and to enable his own servant to answer all just demands that might be made upon me; and, bless his majesty, in his own time he did.

It came to pass soon after this that a gentleman from Plymouth- dock came to town, and often attended my ministry during his stay; and before he departed he wrote me a very kind letter, inviting me to preach at a meeting at the dock, to which himself and some of his family belonged, and gave me to understand that he thought they had the gospel tolerably clear preached to them. This I considered; and, having formerly had various invitations to go to that part of the country, signed by many persons, I was inclined to go. I have no doubt now but it really was the mind and will of God that I should go. But being sometimes much put to it to get supply in my absence, and the good man's letter intimating that he thought the preacher they had was sound in doctrine, and useful in the work, I thought it best to agree with the old gentleman's request to let their preacher come up and officiate for me in my absence; and this was agreed on, and I took my journey. But, previous to my going down, I had been much grieved and exercised in my mind at seeing the rapid progress of the sentiments and rebellion of Tom Paine; and especially when I saw some simple, God-fearing people much leavened with it.

Never did I see so evil a spirit so rapidly spread before, and I hope I never shall again. Many of the poorer sort neglected all business, and all care for their families, till they brought death into the pot. And many of the real children of God, when they saw that whole families and crowded societies were all moved as the trees of the wood are moved, and that many ministers in the pulpit, and swarms of hypocrites in the pews, were carried away with it, it tarnished not a few in the simplicity of the gospel, and the image of Christ began to be sadly defaced in many; and instead thereof sprung up self-conceit, worldly wisdom, high notions of equality, and a thirst for revenge against all that differed in sentiment from them. Many professing people, as well as others, began to meet together in companies to read the wisdom of Tom Paine, till the strongest union was cemented among them by disaffection to others; wherever it came it preyed upon the very vitals of godliness; filial fear, tenderness of heart, conscience before God, timidity in prayer, self-diffidence, humility, meekness, watchfulness, quietude, peace, diligence in business, zeal for God, and fervor in devotion, seemed to have forsaken many, and not a few that my soul loved were sadly fermented with this leaven of malice and wickedness. Satan cares not what we strive and contend about, so that we do not strive at the straight gate, nor contend for the faith of the saints. When I saw what a hand the devil made, and the advantage he gained by trading with Tom Paine, my soul was grieved and my zeal inflamed against this monopoly of Satan, and God filled me with power and might by his Spirit to oppose it, and the farther I went on in it the more the Word of God opened to me, until he was pleased to show me whereabouts in his Word this trying hour stood.

Much displeasure did I incur at this work; some (like Galatians) who would formerly have parted with their own eyes for me, now viewed me as their greatest enemy for enforcing the clearest truth; not a few hissed like a viper in the gallery, while I was insisting on obedience to him that bruised the serpent's head. About this time I published my sermon on "The Books and the Parchments," and this exasperated many still more, till one would have thought that the former cry of "Hosanna" was now changed into that of "Crucify him, crucify him." But God's servants have a better foundation than either the testimony or the applause of men. I was upon the rock long before either their applause or reproach fell upon me.

In this midst of this bustle, and under this cloud of pleasure, I set off for Plymouth-dock, and the preacher at the dock came up as a supply in my absence. The man was an entire stranger to me, and so he remains still, for to this day I do not know him. When I came to the place I heard that there had been a division and sub-division among the people, which I never knew till then; and during my stay there I had various reports from those of my own chapel, some greatly disgusted at his doctrine, and others as much admiring it; but before I left the place I heard very disagreeable things from a real friend of his own, who was compelled in point of conscience to divulge what he did. This sent me home with a heavy heart; and at my return I saw a wonderful blaze, but I was sure the coals were never taken from the altar of burnt-offering; they were zealously affected, but not well. Wild rant and empty oratory, moving the corrupt affections of depraved nature, produced all these sparks, and many poor souls walked in the light of this fire, and in the sparks that they had kindled; but the light of this flame burns no longer than the audible accents of the orator operate; it all dies before the hearer can reach the threshold of his door; and at a dying hour, and at the midnight cry, the very remembrance of it shall vanish.

When I insisted upon fire from the altar of burnt-offering, and that it appertained to the tribe of Levi, or to them that were joined to the Lord, to burn incense, this brought the whole company of Korah upon me; and if I enforced obedience to rulers for conscience' sake, this stirred up all the disciples of Tom Paine. And now I had need to be made a new sharp threshing instrument, having teeth, to thresh these mountains, and make these hills as chaff, in order to fan them, that the wind might carry them away, and that the whirlwind might scatter them, that those that were left might rejoice in the Lord, and glory in the Holy One of Israel (Isa. xli. 15, 16). And by the good hand of God upon us, we saw every word of this prophecy exactly fulfilled; for as the thresher went on the vermin hissed in the mow, the chaff flew like smoke out of the chimney, while the pure grain fell not to the ground, but under a spirit of meekness consolidated together into one heap, and the rest were scattered in the imagination of their hearts, and soon after not less than fifteen were in their graves. While it pleased God to continue me at this work of threshing, the Holy Ghost spoke these words to my heart: "Shall not God avenge his own elect? A word spoken in due season, how good is it?" I thanked my God, and took courage still to labor at threshing the mountains, expecting more wheat as soon as the chaff was gone; for I had not a single doubt but I should still prophesy upon the thick boughs. In this I was not disappointed of my hopes, nor were my expectations cut off; for, when the floor was purged, those that were scattered sent for this new standard-bearer up, with many promises of fidelity. But those who are false to the true riches are never true to the unrighteous mammon, for they abode less time under him than they did under me. And sure I am that this work was of God; for some few among us, who were much looked up to as something more than men, were now looked away from as being less than nothing; others, who had some exalting notions of their own self-sufficiency to tread out the corn, set up a prayer-meeting as an introduction to the pulpit; but, not succeeding in this, with shame they took the lowest room; while many poor honest souls, who could read only the Bible before, now learned to read men; and not a few, who long had appeared all meekness and placidity, lost that garb, and the envy in their bosom never suffered them to put it on again. In the storm I had a five hundred pound debt upon the chapel, and many, filled with envy, prophesied that I should carry that burden to my grave; but all men know not the thoughts of the Lord. I one day, sitting on my chair in the chapel, asked the Almighty what I had done to these men, wherein I had misled them, or whom I had wronged. And the Spirit of God answered, "When they shall make an end to deal treacherously, thou shalt deal treacherously with them" (Isa. xxxiii. I). And so it fell out, for not a few acted the parts of Sanballat and Tobiah; when they grew weary and ashamed of hindering the work, turned about and offered to assist in building; but there is little trust to be put in men whose hearts are not fixed trusting in God.

Chapter XII.

WHILE NUMBERS WERE REJOICING at the thinness of the congregation, and at the apparent diminution of my income, God moved the hearts of my friends to contribute among themselves to clear off the debt of the chapel; they gave me near four hundred pounds, and in a little time after a person left me two hundred more by will. This at once cleared the whole debt, and left me something in hand. It is a bad wind that blows good to none. By this fanning wind God not only purged the floor, but my debt also; for many of the Lord's people, who stood for some time amazed at the strange flame, and as it were halting between two opinions, were brought to a conclusion, by seeing how soon the candle of the wicked went out; it was quenched at once, and we heard no more of it, and then the affections of the people came back to me; which put me in Paul's path of experience, when he said, "But I rejoice in the Lord greatly, that now at last your care for me hath flourished again" (Phil. iv. 10), for they even spoke to the gentleman to whom I sold my books, and he sold them back to them, and contributed handsomely himself; they not only subscribed to buy the books, but raised a fund to reprint some that were out of print. God hath given us all things in Christ. "For your shame you shall have double, and for confusion they shall rejoice in their portion; therefore in their land they shall possess double; everlasting joy shall be unto them" (Isa. lxi. 7). I had long entreated the Lord to remove this load from my shoulders; and "by terrible things in righteousness did the God of my salvation answer me; who is the confidence of all the ends of the earth, and of them that are afar off upon the sea" (Ps. lxv. 5).

But the good hand of my God stopped not here. I had told the whole company that rose up against me, and that publicly in the chapel, that so far from their being able to pull me down, they must not wonder to see me in my coach when old age came on me; nor was the hand of God withdrawn till this came to pass. Upon the house I then lived in, and on the gardens, I had not expended less than three hundred pounds. My lease was only for the term of seven years; but as I gave the landlord all the rent he asked, and paid it punctually every quarter, I had no doubt he was contented with his tenant; yea, so much so that he wished me to get a tenant that I liked to occupy the other house which joined to mine; and moreover told a friend who paid him my rent, that I might prolong my lease whenever I would, so that I thought myself secure enough. But this is not the first time that I have trusted in man, in whom there is no help. It fell out that one night, while I was at Bolney in Sussex, I had a dream: I dreamed that I was standing in my yard at the back side of my house, and all of a sudden I saw my house fall to the ground; it fell with the front downwards, and in my dream I saw it when it was down, and I stood neither alarmed nor concerned about it; and soon I awoke, and behold it was a dream. And as I seemed so composed about the fall of it, I thought that neither me nor my family would be hurt by this fall, whatever it meant. The next morning, at breakfast, I told the gentleman's family, at whose house I was, the dream; but we could make nothing of it. When I returned home, my wife informed me that my landlord had been to inquire after me; and in a day or two he came again to inform me that he was going to sell his houses. I desired him to bring a builder, and I would get another, and they two should value the house. To this he agreed. But instead of two builders meeting, he brought up an auctioneer, who set the price of my house at nine hundred pounds; whereas, not many years before, both of them were sold for four hundred pounds; and at that time they were let for twenty pounds a year each. The auction came on, and they were sold; and if I remember right, my house fetched six hundred guineas, and the other four hundred and fifty pounds, my improvements made that difference. My lease being nearly out, I had another habitation to seek, and went two days, but in vain, as I wanted some rural and retired spot. A few friends, seeing the lease of my present residence advertised to be sold, went (unknown to me) to see it, and much approved of it.

After my friends had been once or twice to see the house they informed me of it, and advised me to go and see it; which I did; but the concern appeared so weighty that I set myself against it to the utmost, remembering my former affliction and my misery, the wormwood and the gall; nor was there one in all my family who approved of it but wife, the distance appeared so far from town. However, my friends mightily pressed me to it; and as the time drew nigh when the lease was to be sold, they determined to attend the sale. I prayed day and night that they might not succeed in buying it, and charged them to bid no higher than thirty pounds; but they resolved among themselves to bid to seventy pounds. It was put up at five pounds, and there was not one bidder till one of my friends bid the five pounds, and it was knocked down to him. At this time I had another dream. I dreamed I was in a large room, and the room was full of serpents, and the bodies of the serpents were divided at the middle and so each of them had two necks and two heads; and many of them crawled furiously up to me open-mouthed, but not one of them bit me; nor was I at all terrified at them. I awaked, and behold it was a dream. But, when I came to see the person that I had to deal with, the dream come fresh into my mind. I saw the serpent, and I had no doubt but that there were more heads than one; yea, many in union with him. There are serpents, and a generation of vipers; and Christ says they are of their father. And never, in this world, did I see so great a likeness of him.

The things on the premises were to be taken by an appraisement; the good man was to chose [*sic*] one, and I the other. I had, in my own mind, fixed upon one in much practice; and, had I made choice of him, I should have added a third head to the crooked fraternity. But this was not to be. My God will have a hand in all my affairs; and I was directed by him to inquire after another of great note, one who stood very high and honorable in his profession. And this gentleman was well acquainted with the reptile that I had to deal with. The gentleman that he employed went through the work first, and the person who was for me soon went after him; and, when they met upon the business, they could not agree together so as to settle the affairs. During which time my kind friend with two heads very politely offered me possession of the premises, and urged the necessity of it, as the second crop of grass was fit to cut, which I well knew, and took it very kindly of him from one of his heads; but I could not take my eye from the other, being not ignorant of Satan's devices; and, suspecting that I must be brought to submit to any terms after I had taken possession, I therefore declined it till the matters could be properly adjusted. The principal matter in debate was respecting a small quantity of manure, worth about six pounds, and which, according to the tenor of the lease, should have been laid on the land before that period. My appraiser would not allow me to pay for that, and at last he carried his point; and, striking the dung and other matters off from the inventory, they both agreed, and for the stock and fixtures I paid three hundred and seventy pounds; and then took possessions with all the formalities and punctilios of human laws, my attorney and friends being present with me.

And now I must beg my dearly beloved friend's pardon for digressing a little from my intended subject, in order to pursue this wriggling family a little farther, and to convince you that what God showed me in a vision he afterwards showed me in reality; or, to speak more plainly, I really saw with my bodily eyes those very creatures creeping upon the earth, which at first appeared only in imagination; for I had not been long in possession of my new habitation before I received a squib, or rather a cracker, for there were many folds and doubles in its meaning. It came from an honest lawyer. The contents were "That he was absent from town at the settling of our affairs; that the notion of not paying for the dung was a false one; and that, if he had been at the meeting, his client should have been paid. And farther, he wished to know what I thought of the matter. This opened the monstrous mystery of *two heads* a little more plainly.

A secret something within told me to take no notice of this. I showed the letter to Father Green; and Mrs. Green said she knew the honest lawyer well, and spoke very highly of his wisdom in his profession, telling me that her former husband, who died a member with us, had lent a person twenty pounds; and as the borrower proved a villain, her husband employed this honest attorney to recover the money; but he never recovered one farthing of it, only brought in a bill of twenty pounds more for his trying, or not trying, to get it. And surely, if the unjust steward in the gospel, for reducing the debts of his lord's debtors to nearly half the amount, be commended because he had done wisely, this good man had a right to the same honor; for he just doubled the debt, and got the same sum of his client for himself that the debtor had cheated him of before. But to return. The silent contempt that I poured upon this three-and-fourpenny squib brought another scrap of the same price, "desiring to know where my attorney lived, that, as I chose to remain silent and come to no terms, he might debate the matter with him," etc. I took the wise man's counsel; I still held my peace, that I might be esteemed a man of understanding; for "he that openeth wide his lips (in such cases) shall have destruction" (Prov. xiii. 3). Soon after I was served with a something, I know not what, as it was a text that I had never handled; but I remember one of the heads of the subject was "forty pounds for dung." After some little trouble of collecting witnesses and some few materials together, it came into Westminster Hall. My antagonist seemed quite in his element. Courts of law were his sunny banks, where he folded himself in many a coil, and raised his crest to such a height, that he was heard by my friends to say that he knew law enough for twenty men. I would to God that he had been taught a few lessons from the old lawgiver of the Jews. Moses would have made him talk less and do more. However, these laws are still to be learned, and must be learned, sooner or later, by all the offspring of Adam, at the last and grand assize.

When the matter came into court his counsellor began to open his mouth, and to go on with the business, till the venerable judge stopped him, telling him he need not proceed, for he had no foundation to go upon, and showed his reason for it, and added, "You must nonsuit him."

Here it ended for the present; but soon after I heard that he obtained a something, but I know not what, from the twelve judges. It was to try this matter over again, and to collect more forces for the trial. All this time I kept my eye upon my dream. I saw the creatures, and their mouths open; and I know that the scriptures say of the king of Babylon, "Shall they not rise up suddenly that shall bite thee, and awake that shall vex thee, and thou shalt be for booties unto them?" (Hab ii. 7). And this is what I wanted to know, whether God would suffer these to bite as well as vex, and at last to make a booty of me. In my dream they did not.

After a time this trial came on again, and then a young man stepped forth, and swore, and said that the two appraisers could not, and did not, settle the matter, but it was left to be settled between me and my antagonist. This was another of the crooked ones. At which time the counsel for me gave the young man the inventory, and asked him who wrote that on the back of it? He replied, after some time, that he himself did. And the words were, "This is to certify that no one thing crossed out in this inventory is to be paid for." Signed by himself. The venerable lord cried out, "Villany [sic] indeed!" Here it ended, with all cost and suit on his shoulders who wore the two heads. And I was informed that it cost the crooked one two hundred and seventy pounds. And all this time I was not once bitten. God speaks once, yea twice, in dreams, in visions, by his judgments, by his providence, by his Son, by his Spirit, and sometimes by his servants; but, let him speak however he may, I set to my seal that God is true.

I must now prepare my stuff for removing. For some few years before I was married all my personal effects used to be carried in my hand, or on my shoulders, in one or two large handkerchiefs; but, after marriage, for some few years, I used to carry all the goods that we had gotten on my shoulders in a large sack. But, when we moved from Thames Ditton to London, we loaded two large carts with furniture and other necessaries, besides a post-chaise well filled with children. But at this time God had given me such treasure in my sack that it was increased to a multitude; we were almost a fortnight in getting away the stuff. The many things on the premises which I had to purchase, and the expenses that would attend my moving, together with rent for both houses for some time to come, had previously exercised my mind not a little. And I have always kept Claremarket, but never did any business at the Stocks-market in my life, so that I could not look there for any supply. But I looked to the market in Honey Lane; for his word has often been sweeter to me than honey or the honeycomb, for it contains the promise of the life that now is, and of that which is to come; and here I never sought, I never looked, I never prayed in vain. God raised me up a most invaluable friend, who richly supplied me, and had long ministered to my necessities. But the trouble of moving drove me quite out of my element; it interrupted my peace, scattered my thoughts, and prevented all meditation. The door of hope seemed to be off the hooks, and the best members of the new man out of joint. I appeared quite unfurnished for the pulpit, and my mind too unsettled for any one branch of my delightful labor. "No man that warreth entangleth himself with the affairs of this life," says Paul; and sad entanglements are all worldly concerns to a spiritual soldier. But if this world, and the domestic concerns of it, are a burden and not a pleasure, a vanity and not a substance, a vexation and not a delight, a rival and not a real lover, we must of course be crucified to it, and alive to Him that was crucified in it.

Being in some measures settled in my new habitation, I watched, and sought, and felt, after that Friend that loveth at all times; and, blessed be his revered name, I found him. If I had failed in this I had been undone, for he is our dwelling-place in all generations; and sensible sinners have no sure dwelling nor quiet resting-place but this. But now many cares came on me. I was five miles from my chapel, and a cold winter was coming on; and how to get my family so far to the house of God was my chief concern. A person of Streatham, in Surrey, had made me a present of a little sorrel horse, which is a most excellent creature, and would carry me very well; but how to get a large family there was the difficulty. A man and his wife with whom I have been for some years acquainted at Streatham, and who had managed a farm for a gentleman there had been for some time before this out of employ, through the gentleman's letting his farm. I had spoken to two friends in London about joining with me in taking a farm, and putting him into it to manage it for us, for the sake of a dairy, etc., to supply our three families; but we could not hear of any such thing near town that would do for that purpose. The man and his wife therefore took a coal shed, and dealt in green grocery, etc., etc. But I found, by inquiry, that their business was not likely to answer, and therefore I sent for the man to come to me; and he and his wife agreed to come, she to attend to my baking and dairy, and he to the business of the land. And here God granted me my request in a way that I did not expect; for being long acquainted with them, and they being fond of my ministry, I did not like to see them scattered from it. I had got one old cart-horse that I had bought with the rest of the stock on the farm, and I wanted two more, but money ran short; and I determined also to have a large tilted cart to take my family to chapel, and the man should drive it on the Sunday, and on lecture nights, and I would ride my little horse. This was the most eligible plan that I could adopt; and on this I determined, as soon as God should send money to procure them. I came to this conclusion on Friday, and on the next day, toward evening, came two or three friends from town to see me. I wondered not a little at their coming, as they knew that on a Saturday I never like to see any body; and therefore I conceived that they must be come with some heavy tidings; some friend was dead, or something bad had happened. But they came to inform me that some friends had agreed among themselves and bought me a coach and a pair of horses, which they intended to make me a present of. I informed them that the assessed taxes ran so high that I should not be able to keep it. But they stopped my mouth by informing me that the money for paying the taxes for the coach and horses was subscribed also; so that nothing lay upon me but the keep of the horses. Thus, instead of being at the expense of a tilted cart, God sent me a coach without cost, and two horses without my purchasing them; and which, with my other old horse, would do the work of the farm, as well as the work of the coach; and my bailiff informed me that he could drive it, having formerly drove one. Thus was I set up. But at this time the pocket was bare, and many things were wanting, both in the house and on the farm, and a place to fit up for my bailiff and dairy woman to live in. And it was but a few days afterward before a gentleman out of the country called upon me; and, being up in my study with me, he said, "My friend, I often told you that you would keep your coach before you died, and I always promised that whenever you had a coach I would give you a pair of horses, and I will not be worse than my word. I have inquired of father Green, and he tells me that the horses cost forty-five pounds; and there is the money." In a day or two after the coach, horses, and harness, came. And, having now a little money, I wrote to a friend in the country to send me twelve ewes, and a male with them; and they sent me twelve excellent ones, and the males with them, but would not be paid for them; they were a present to the farm. "Whoso is wise, and will observe these things, even they shall understand the loving kindness of the Lord" (Ps. cvii. 43).

When my coach came home, and my family had been once or twice to chapel in it, and the report of it was gone abroad, it was truly laughable to see the sorrow, the hard labor, and sore travail that fell upon some poor souls on the account of it. Their envy almost slew the silly ones. One person came into my yard and asked the coachman about this matter, and what all these things meant; but he being a stranger who came with the coach, and only drove us two or three times, could not inform him. Others, and some very well dressed gentlemen, whom I knew nothing of, and whom I never saw before, came and walked at different times to and fro at the front of the house by the hour together, looking up, and then down, to consider the matter, and to find out what it all proceeded from, which is a mystery they can never get at; and the mystery of God's providential dealings is what I never shall be able to describe. I can only look on and wonder at God, while others wonder at me, and say with the Psalmist, "I am a wonder unto many, but thou art my strong refuge" (Ps. lxxi. 7).

We have had some of these envious ones stand in convocation in the by-road which leads to Hendon, and hold a council, and debate upon the matter for hours together; what the rent is, what the taxes, the number of the family, the keep of the horses and servants, the taxes of the house, coach, etc., and what must unavoidably be the amount of the whole, yearly, while Mr. Williams stood on the other side of the wall and heard the debates and the conclusion. And here they took more pains than ever I did, for I never once cast up either the income or outgoings till the income tax was made; only I observed this, that the income seldom trod upon the heels of the outgoings. There was generally a little space between them, and in that gap I erected my watch-tower, and in which ward I have sometimes been whole nights, when other folks have been in bed and asleep. At the chapel door also we were not a little troubled with this sort of well-wishers, sometimes twenty or more, about the coal-heaver's state coach, to examine matters, and to look into things. And this continued, more or less, for near two years. Indeed, it is but lately that this wonder of wonders has begun to cease. And yet my friends, who executed all this business for me, took care to give them all the information that malice itself could expect; for the initials of my name, W. H., together with the initials of my state, S. S., were put upon every panel of the coach, upon the pads of the harness, and upon the very blindfolds of the bridles. And all this was done to satisfy those who were the principal mourners on this occasion that the thing was real, and not counterfeit; that it was not a hackney carriage, nor a glass coach; not borrowed, nor hired, nor a job; but the despised doctor's own carriage, which the King of kings had sent him without asking for, and, at that time, without any expectation of any such thing.

And here I have often thought of the words of the sweet psalmist of Israel. When he, and the four hundred troops that were with him, all of whom were in desperate circumstances, such as were in distress, those that were discontented, and such as were in debt, these only joining him (I Sam. xxii. 2), and while he and this handful of men wandered in the wilderness, and in the woods, in caves, in rocks, and in strong holds, like Robin Hood and Little John in the forest of Sherwood, Nabal's shepherds, as appears by his famous speech to Abigail, all who knew them, and all laboring and husbandmen about these wild places were conversant with them, and not a few of the heathen, as the Philistines also; but when the report was spread that this wood-ranger was crowned king in Hebron, and his desperate followers were the life-guards of his royal person in that city of Israel, then they gathered themselves together, and went in troops to see the sight; and when they saw the crown royal and the purple robe upon the son of Jesse, they assembled in different assemblies, and compassed him about; yea, the objects gathered themselves together; they walked round about the walls of his palace, and fretted at his exaltation. And he seems to take notice of it, and says, "They make a noise like a dog, and go round about the city." And, as it seemed to amuse them, David desired that they might be permitted to continue at it, and therefore adds, "And at evening let them return; and let them make a noise like a dog, and go round about the city. Let them wander up and down for meat, and grudge if they be not satisfied" (Ps. lix. 6, 14, 15).

And here I must mention one or two particulars which have often been a wonder to me. And one is, when I came first to reside in London I brought my poor old gray horse to town with me, and being not able to keep him, a friend of mine and a dear son in the faith, who kept a livery stable, took him till he could be sold; and during this time, a gentleman asked me to take a ride with him a little way in the country, and we went up Edgware road, a road I had never been before, and turned up toward Hampstead; and I particularly observed one house in the way, with the garden, walls, and the summer-house, and a few fir trees which were about it. And, being in the summer, I observed to the gentleman that was with me what a retired, rural spot it was; and it seemed to take my fancy, and to catch my eye, more than any other that we observed; and that very house is now my residence.

The next particular is this: About four years ago I was invited to preach at Woolwich, and I engaged a few friends to go with me, and begged of father Green to get some stable keeper to furnish us a rich coach and horses for the day. He replied that he knew a man of the name of Nibbs who kept coaches, and who generally drove himself, and who was a very civil man, and had a large family; and I remember we loaded the coach very heavily; and, when we came to Woolwich, I ordered the good man who owned the horses to feed them to the full, and it should be at my expense. Toward the evening it thundered, lightened and rained at a most violent rate, and the road was very wet and slippery, and being above the common number for a coach to take, I had a good deal of feeling for the poor cattle; and, before I got in, I went and looked at the horses, to see their size and weight, and what state they were in, whether poor or in working order; whether decrepit or sound; and whether they looked full or empty; and I much admired the team. They were both grays, and the shape or mould of one of them much took my eye; he was a dapple gray, very spotted, and of the tabby cast. And, the team much pleasing me, I desired the master of them to drive slow, and not to hurt his cattle, and, as we were a heavy load, we would reward him, which we did to his satisfaction. And that horse which so forcibly struck my eye is one of the pair which my friends bought for me, and is now in my team. Some gentleman in town having often seen him in my cart, and afterwards in the coach, took a fancy to him, and made many inquiries whose he was, and at last inquired of the hackneyman where he came from, who informed him, and who, by the gentleman's desire, came to purchase him; and others also have bid for him, but he is still with me. God's gifts are not to be parted with but in case of necessity. Thus the man that I wished to put on a farm now drives me, the house I then saw, which so much took my fancy, is my residence, and the horse I took such notice of is now in my team.

I often looked back, with many tears, at the undeserved and unexpected mercy of my God, and with the joys of a good hope, through grace, that I should one day see him whom my soul loves. And with much delight did my soul exult in my bountiful Benefactor; and not without a lasting sense of his undeserved love to me, from which alone all real gratitude of heart flows; for all which I am deeply indebted to his free and super-abounding grace. This frame of mind, and my bodily infirmities, kept my temporal prosperity in its proper place, as a nice handmaid, under God, to assist my faith, but not to become a snare; and it likewise kept my mind heavenly, and rather assisted me for the pulpit than otherwise; for the more we see his goodness the more boldly we proclaim it. "Out of the abundance of the heart the mouth speaketh."

Chapter XIII.

IT NOW FELL OUT that I was earnestly invited to go a journey into the North to preach; but, having the gout in my pocket, I was obliged to postpone it till I was loosed from this infirmity; and when the cure came the cold winterly weather was come on. However, I sent to my friends of whom I had my coach, and begged the loan of a chariot. These friends supply me gratis with a chariot or chaise, or any light carriage that I may want, whenever I ask. They sent the chariot, and off I went, with about eleven pounds in my pocket, which small sum I knew would require more frugality than I am master of to go so long a journey. However, I set off in style with this small capital; and, having been long expected by some of the Lord's tried ones, and they having now despaired of my coming, except one or two, upon whose minds it was impressed that I should come, just before my letter of information reached them; which delay sharpened their appetites. One poor soul had her work sweetly revived; another young woman, who had been long in chains, came forth to the light, and showed herself; and, had my hand been as open as their hearts, they had sent me home with thirty guineas in my pocket; but I returned some of it back again, knowing it is more blessed to give than to receive. God threw my heart quite open when He first revealed His dear Son in me, and the transforming views that I have at times been favored with since has kept it open to this day, so that I keep clear-market all the year round; as it comes in, so it goes out, so that neither my heart nor my pocket are standing pools, but springing wells; and not a few mumping professors and lazy hypocrites have made an easy prey of me, the devil artfully instructing his fraternity to fish after the tender feelings of those whose hearts have been made soft by heavenly discipline. But of late I have found myself better armed against these drone-bees than formerly. When my bounty goes into the family of God I fret not; but it hurts my consequence to be duped by the devil in a serpent, or a wolf in a sheep's skin.

Soon after my return from this journey I discharged some small debts; for God seldom sends me one guinea till that guinea is owing, or wanted immediately some other way. He has strictly preserved this uniform and unalterable method with me, now near upon twenty-eight years, without ever deviating in the least from it; for, when he cleared the debts of the chapel, there were several small debts for other things left unpaid; so that the little overplus was soon demanded. And the general method of his proceedings with me are, that when his hand has been for some time closed till my debts are greatly increased, then the devil is let loose upon me, who is suffered to bring them all to my view, one after another, even from a fifty pound debt down to a shilling. This sets me to looking up and praying to God; soon after which my creditors and their demands are banished from my mind, and at which time faith springs up, fully persuading me that the raven, or the hand-basket, is on the road, which is as sure to come as faith is to proclaim its coming.

But I must now return to the time of my returning from the north country. I before observed that some small debts were then discharged. But soon after this, the hand of God was fast closed again, of which I am as sensible as I am of the heat of the sun. This continued for some time; and for all that time I watched and observed it narrowly. And at this time there was a debt due of twenty pounds; though it was never asked for or demanded, yet I knew it was due. It was for tithes; for, though I am a gentleman of the cloth myself, yet, being not a regular, but an ir-regular, I am constrained to pay tithes, offerings, dues, and fees, though I live upon nothing but offerings my-self, and these are neither few nor small.

I looked different ways, and chalked out different roads, for the Almighty to walk in; but his paths were in the deep waters, and his footsteps were not known. No raven came, neither in the morning nor in the evening. There was a gentlewoman at my house on a visit, and I asked her if she had got the sum of twenty pounds in her pocket, telling her, at the same time, how much I wanted it. She told me she had not; if she had I should have it. A few hours after the same woman was coming into my study, but she found it locked, and knocked at the door. I let her in, and she said, "I am sorry I disturbed you." I replied, "You do not dis-turb me; I have been begging a favor of God, and I had just done when you knocked; and that favor I have now got in faith, and shall shortly have in hand, and you will see it." The afternoon of the same day two gentlemen out of the city came to see me; and, after a few hours' conversation they left me, and, to my great surprise, each of them, at parting, put a letter into my hand, which, when they were gone, I opened, and found a ten pound note in each. I immediately sent for the woman upstairs, and let her read the letters, and then sent the money to answer that demand.

About this time an affair happened which I do not care to pass over. I had a few very fine pigs in my yard, and a neighbor of mine had the misfortune to lose one. To repair his loss I made him a present of one of mine. Two more very poor men in the country, who are obliged to live by faith as well as myself, wanted each of them a pig to keep for the winter, and I made each of them a present of one. A person being sick in the house desired a bit of one, and I ordered one to be killed; and soon after that, a sudden death happened to another; so that I was obliged to buy two, which cost me five guineas, and not so good as my own. A day or two after this, when I went home, I saw seven fat sheep and a fat lamb in my field. I asked my man where they came from. He said he knew not. "Last night," said he, "a man brought them, and I told him he had brought them to the wrong place, for I had bought none, and I was sure my master had bought none; and therefore I desired him to take them back again." The man replied, "Is this Mr. Huntington's house?" The answer was, "Yes, it is." "Then," said the man, "my orders were to drive them here; and here I will leave them, nor will I drive them anywhere else." And the man was right.

Another sad calamity presented itself, and that was the extravagant price of oats, and four horses to keep; and, though my favorite young horse has been coveted by several, yet I did not care to part with him; for if I have any hobbies in this world, they are most certainly my gardens and my living creatures. Besides, to sell a horse would look as if the Doctor was sinking in the world. And, to add to all this, the Philistines had lately been upon me; I mean the tax-gatherers. I am never spared upon this head. I pay some pounds per annum poor's-rates, even for the chapel; and upon my appealing to the higher powers to know the cause, a wise man informed me that chapels were nothing but shops, and Lord Mansfield had declared it; and therefore it must be true. However, many gentlemen are much in the dark about the goods that we shopkeepers deal in; for, had they ever bought either wine or milk without money and without price, they would set more value upon such a shop than they would upon the Bank of England or the Royal Exchange.

I really believe it has pleased God to raise me up and send me forth, not only into the ministry, that I might tell them that fear God what he hath done for my soul; but it hath pleased him to keep me depending on his providence, from hand to mouth, throughout the whole course of my pilgrimage, that I might publish to the church at large, not a recital of what Providence has done for others, but, as a living witness of the facts, what he has done for me, to encourage the faith of others. And God has so done it that infidelity itself cannot give this my testimony the lie; for these things were not done in a corner. The persons whom God hath raised up and made use of to assist me in times of need, being in number about five hundred brethren, are all witnesses of these facts, for of these "the greater part remain unto this present, but some are fallen asleep." Nor have I a single doubt but it is the will of God that I should publish these things. Of this I have had a most glaring proof but this week; for after I had begun this narrative, and wrote about two thirds of it, I got weary of it, and cold to it, and laid it aside for two or three months, and seemed to have no inclination to meddle with it any more. But, at the beginning of last week, I had several debts brought to my mind, and set continually before me, and being at the same time under my often infirmity, the gout in the pocket (I call it the gout; for, when I have got a little money, I am for going here and there into the country to visit the brethren, and see how they do; but, when my infirmity is upon me, I am confined to my work in town); seeing several debts set before my eyes, and being at the same time afflicted with this disorder, God's hand being quite shut up ever since I returned from Lewes, I cast matters over in my mind, and said, What shall I do? The answer was, Sit down and finish your Bank of Faith, and God will bless the sale of it, and that will answer present demands. And, although every circumstance here related was entirely gone both from my mind and memory, having laid it so long aside, and having no heart to meddle with it again, yet, when I came to a determination to shut myself up in town all day long to write, and went to bed with this determination, I no sooner awaked in the morning but almost every circumstance that is related in these fifty or sixty latter pages of the work were all brought to my mind, and set in order before me, so that I had nothing to do but to sit down and write them off hand; and no sooner had I begun but I found my soul remarkably happy, and much delighted in the work; and I believe the whole of this was done by that sweet Remembrancer who is to bring all things to our remembrance whatsoever Jesus Christ has spoken unto us, whether by chastisements or by comforts, by frowns or by smiles, or providence or in grace (John xiv. 26).

Moreover, when I have come to some particulars, which I have thought would be disclosing all my secret conflicts to some that hate me, and be an entertainment to those who feed upon ashes, and little better than casting pearls before swine, and rather hurt the consequence of the Doctor than otherwise, a resolution to seek God's honor and his people's good before my own, has been attended with sensible sensations of heavenly comfort, insomuch that my mouth has been often filled with laughter while I have been writing them.

Some little time ago I was invited to preach at a distance from London, the minister of the place being sick. It was some time before I could raise the wind, or furnish the pocket for this expedition. However, at last it came in, though I forgot the quarter it came from; and with about ten pounds I set off, and stayed over two Sabbath days. Just before my departure, a gentleman gave me six guineas, another ten, and two others gave me five guineas each. Another pressed me hard with a farther present, which I refused, being full and abounding. So true is the word of God. Where God uses a servant of his to sow spiritual things bountifully, carnal things are as bountifully reaped; and in both senses, they that sow sparingly reap sparingly. "The liberal soul deviseth liberal things, and by liberal things shall he stand." That text hath often been a support and a comfort to me; and I can set to my seal that God is true.

But I come now to a disaster which befel [*sic*] me. My young horse fell sick about two months ago, and so he continues to be, with little likelihood of his ever recovering. A valuable cow, which cost me fifteen pounds, fell ill, and wasted to a skeleton. My man said that her inside was decayed, so we parted with her for fifty shillings. About this time a dog came in the night and killed a lamb, and ate up almost the whole of it. Three nights after he came again, and killed five capital ewes, and wounded another lamb. From that time two men, well armed, watched for three or four nights, when, about one o'clock in the morning, the dog came again. They both fired at him, and both hit him, and brought him down. He was a terrible creature, of the lurcher and wolf kind; but he met with his just deserts. I have just received a lawyer's letter demanding payment for the dog. All these things are against me.

But not many days after this the Lord sent me, by different hands, twenty-seven pounds ten shillings, and thus repaired my loss. Poor Jacob had many of his flock torn by wild beasts, and some stolen by day and some by night; and Laban made him bear the loss of them all; but God's blessing upon him always repaired his losses; and though his wages were changed ten times, he went home to his country two bands. I have often observed that in whatever we take the most delight, there the calamity generally falls. I long since saw this in the death of four or five of my children, and I see it now; for it is my favorite horse that is sick, and my little flock, that are the principal part of my hobby; and it is among these that the slaughter was made.

I must now drop a few observations that I have made upon Providence, which I hope will not be tedious or disagreeable to my dearly beloved friend; I mean with respect to such things as have often appeared to fulfil the desires of my heart when I dared not, when I could not muster up courage enough to ask or pray for them. For instance: soon after my deliverance I went to hear the word at Kingston upon Thames, where I sometimes heard a gentleman from London who was something of an orator; and his oratory had such an effect upon me that I often wished I had but property enough, I would carry that person at my own expense all over the nation, that he might spread the gospel of the Saviour in every place. And yet I never got any comfort or establishment from his ministry, but the contrary; for I was sure to return home in legal bondage whenever I heard him. This served to give me a little insight into the deception and vanity of human oratory without the power of divine grace. Now, though I never dared to ask the Almighty for riches to enable me thus to do, yet he soon afterwards opened my mouth to tell others what he had done for me; and it hath pleased God to give testimony to the word of his grace. And thus "the desires of the righteous shall be granted" (Prov. x. 24).

Another thing I much desired was that I might be

enabled to build a house of prayer for the Lord, to show the love and regard I had to him for his manifold mercies to me, though I never dared to ask God to enable me to do any such thing. Yet it fell out about two or three years afterwards that a person at Worpolsdon, near Guildford in Surrey, offered to give a bit of ground and an old barn, and to secure it for the good of the Lord's cause, if I could collect the sum of forty pounds to build a chapel. I did so, and the place was soon erected; but the person who took upon himself to see the writing executed and the place secured, neglected it; and soon after, the man on whose ground the place was built lost his wife, and taking a liking to a woman of some property, who was of the Baptist persuasion, went into the water; and after that the place was taken away from me, and a Baptist minister admitted in my room, where he continued but a few weeks, for most of the people followed me to another place.

Before I was turned out of this little chapel, the Lord showed me what was coming on, and sent me these two passages of Scripture: "Because he hath oppressed and hath forsaken the poor; because he hath violently taken away an house which he buildeth not; surely he shall not save of that which he desired" (Job xx. 19, 20). And, "Whoso rewardeth evil for good, evil shall not depart from his house" (Prov. xvii 13). Previous to my being turned out of the chapel I opened my thoughts and views to the person on whose ground the chapel was built, and told him all that I saw coming on, as it respected himself; that he was going to be married; that he must go into the water before the woman would have him; and that afterwards he would take the place from me. And in this I believe I told him all the intentions of his heart. He wept, and said, "God forbid!" But very soon afterwards he fulfilled the prediction. And when I received my orders to come there no more, I told him that evil would never depart from his house. To which he replied, "It is a light thing to be judged of you, or of man's judgment." However, soon afterwards God sent an evil spirit among the few that abode there, and divided and scattered them into all winds. The premises were sold, and my little chapel was sold also, for a place to put corn in. Nor did that man every prosper afterwards as long as he lived; and he died a few years after this affair happened.

We afterwards built a little place at Working [*sic*] in Surrey, and I collected about twenty-five pounds towards that; and the Word is preached there to this day. Soon after I collected about forty pounds towards building one at Sunbury at Middlesex; and not long after the Lord enabled me to build Providence chapel in London. In these things God fulfilled the desires of my heart, though I could not muster up courage to pray for them.

Furthermore, I long wished to have a situation where there was plenty of garden-ground, as I understood gardening, and found that buying garden stuff for a large family took a deal of money. And it has pleased my God to grant me this also. "He will fulfill the desire of them that fear him" (Ps. cxlv. 19).

I must mention two more of the desires of my heart, if my dear friend is not weary of these things. I much wished for a place with two or three acres of land, being desirous of keeping a cow, as there is no such thing as good milk to be got in London, and milk is a very useful article in a large family. I aimed no higher than a dairy of one cow, and for years tried to get such a situation, and had nearly accomplished it once, by taking a house in Cravon-hill, near Bayswater, but was disappointed, and therefore gave up all expectations of it. But not long after I was settled where I now am, and instead of one cow, the Lord sent me four.

Once more. Preaching once a week in the city, it often

happened in the winter season that it rained or snowed on the nights of my being there. At such times it was seldom that a hackney-coach could be got, being generally all taken up; so that I was obliged frequently to walk to Paddington. And not a few deplorable wet journeys have I had of this sort, which made me often wish that my circumstances would enable me to engage a glass-coach statedly for two or three nights in the week. But how this desire was granted, and exceeded by the gift of the coach and horses, I have related before.

And here ends the narrative of this remarkable man. While God does not call every man to this special mode of life, yet all may learn from it the great importance of a simple trust in God for help in every time of need. The want of such a faith has brought clouds and darkness upon many a soul, and its possession has carried many through rough places in holy triumph. "Have faith in God," is the divine command, for "all things are possible to him that believeth."